DEDICATION

To Lou:
Veterans and hard workers like you make our country
great. Thanks for the privilege to call you a friend.

D0169624

TABLE OF CONTENTS

SHOW UP

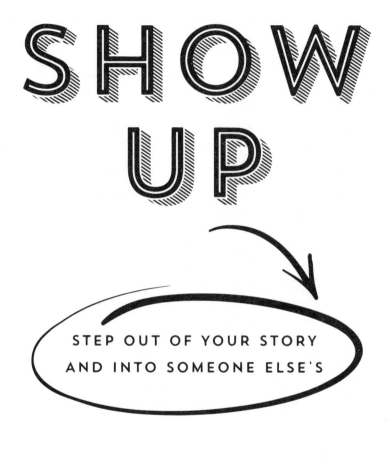

STEP OUT OF YOUR STORY
AND INTO SOMEONE ELSE'S

DAVID STAAL

dustjacket · MEADOWS EDGE GROUP

🕮 dustjacket

www.dustjacket.com

C H A P T E R   1

SLOW DOWN AND SHOW UP

We enter this life created to connect with one another. In fact, we arrive with a variety pack of internal instincts and desires in that direction. Without any help or specific training, I developed a genuine longing to hear my name, to feel comfortable at home, and to eat chips with salsa. The core needs inside of you may be quite similar—or they may be very different.

A few, though, are common to all. The standard issue list that everyone receives includes a deep, quasi-magnetic pull toward other people, especially the lonely ones and those in need. Folks seem to unintentionally lose that instinct, though—sometimes temporarily, other times longer. Fortunately, this mysterious attraction patiently waits in the lost and found closet for anyone who wants to claim it. And when that happens, when someone discovers or rediscovers the joy of showing up for another person, a piece of the world works again exactly as it should.

At an early age, our daughter Erin showed a sincere desire to be helpful—in a three-year-old way, of course. "Daddy, can I pour the juice?" she'd ask.

"Okay, but be careful."

"Uh-oh Daddy. Looks like the cup didn't hold enough. Can I clean it up?"

Fortunately, Erin's helpful spirit stayed and grew. Later that same year, she would put it to use in a way that served me well, in a manner that only a three-year-old could ever pull off.

It's hard to explain to a child so young that daddy has cancer. That changed, though, as I went through harsh, daily drug therapy. By the time Erin arrived home from preschool every day, I had gone through nausea, chills, and shakes that ended in high fever. Like an overheated car that ran out of gas, I lay motionless in bed and repeatedly pleaded with God to help me fall asleep. *If I can fall asleep in the next thirty minutes, I think I can make it.*

"Where's Daddy?"

"In bed."

"What's he doing?"

"Trying to take a nap. Let's be quiet because he really needs to sleep but he can't."

Erin sensed that Daddy needed someone to do something to help him. Every afternoon that entire month of treatment, Erin quietly opened the door and with the graceful motions of a tiny ballerina, scampered across the floor and made the short hop up into the bed, landing as gently and quietly as a silk scarf. She then snuggled ever so lightly against me and likely wondered why I felt so hot. It worked; I fell asleep. Prayer answered.

From an early age, conviction exists deep inside us that we can make a tremendous difference for someone else when we physically show up for them. A hug or handshake. An offer to help. An ear to listen. A smile. Sometimes the right words. Other times none at all. For a moment or maybe much longer. Not a phone call. Not a text message. Nothing can replace personal presence. It's something anyone can do—three-year-olds and even us.

Yet some folks outgrow it.

Health issues typically magnify the need for this kind of connection. My most recent experience in that area came thanks to major ankle surgery.

For the first two months, I wheeled around on a scooter with my lower left leg in an immobilizing boot. On flat, level surfaces I steadily increased speed and pushed the limits of turn radius and corner leans. At home and at the office, my motocross-like transportation system worked well. Not the case outdoors, though. Sidewalks and parking lots offer challenges that most never notice. Unanticipated cracks can cause a top-heavy, wheeled device to abruptly stop, causing the driver to momentarily lose control and hop on one leg with the same wobble of a toddler learning to walk. Cute when a kid; ugly as an adult.

My first post-surgery week back to work brought the challenge of independent transportation: drive to destination, curse about the people parked in handicap areas with no permit, find a close spot, hop from the door of my car to the trunk, lift my scooter out, unfold it while balanced on one foot, and then wheel into the building. At day's end, repeat the process in reverse.

My third day back, I scored the parking place across the narrow drive from the front door. Oh what a wonderful day! As I left the building that afternoon, though, my view of the day changed.

A group of men stood immediately outside the double glass doors as I wheeled off the elevator, gaining speed. The church-leader conference taking place on our building's first floor was on break, so a dozen attendees enjoyed the late-summer sun and fresh breeze. I looked forward to rolling down my car windows and doing the very same thing. Only one thing stood between me and the pure enjoyment that awaited—a tight twelve-guy cluster.

Just as my temporary permit entitled me to special parking privileges, you might assume my leg in a heavy toe-to-knee boot wheeling on a four-wheel cart should earn me pedestrian right of way. But as I stood on one leg inside the door, no one moved. Indeed, no one noticed. *Oh well,* I thought, *they'll part after I press the automatic opener—or they'll get hit.*

So both sets of doors opened, which allowed me to wheel ahead. Still no one moved. "Excuse me," I said to avoid contact. Those words bought me enough space to squeeze through and scoot down the tapered sidewalk cement toward my car, only twenty feet ahead. That's when the real challenge arrived.

I opened the trunk fine. The scooter folded up as usual. But as I lifted it, my lone good foot stepped on a stone just large enough to disrupt my balance. Several awkward, loud, almost violent hops followed. I ended up making a final large hop to crash backwards onto the side of my car to regain equilibrium. For a few long and embarrassing moments, I stood still, breathing hard. The scooter still had to go into the trunk.

Yet none of the able-bodied people only a car length away offered help. A few looked over, trying to suppress their laughter. I admit that graceful appears nowhere on my resume, and the scooter/boot combo further depleted my coordination. But c'mon. I clearly needed help and no one made a move toward me. So I made a couple of short, slow hops back to my original position and placed the cart in the trunk. Again, I paused to catch my breath. That's when a nearby voice startled me.

"Sweetie, do you need help?"

"No, I'm okay."

"You don't need to try that little dance again. Here's my arm; let's get you to your door and in your seat."

"Thanks, I appreciate it."

"No biggie. You take it easy."

No, the voice did not belong to any guy from the sidewalk. The good Samaritan who stopped to help me saw my dilemma from a different parking lot area and she walked several hundred feet to lend a hand. (Ironically, the topic for the church leader conference on break was outreach: a topic apparently so interesting to discuss that it trumps the need to actually do anything.) As I sat in my car, with windows now down to regain all my senses before the drive home, I watched the helpful lady walk into the building through the far door—the entrance clients take when they visit the facility's food pantry. She's a person who needs help—and she's a person willing to offer help. The people most eager to show up for someone else often know what needing help feels like.

Although we're hardwired to connect, our society has gone wireless. Why? Look no further than busyness. It's like a firewall that prevents one person from noticing what's happening with another person.

Rather than completely trash the church guys in the parking lot—although I admit to a partial effort in that direction—an inconvenient truth comes to mind. Too many times I've stood still on my side of the street, safely uninvolved. Unsure of what to do and what might happen, I overcomplicate the situation to justify unresponsiveness. Yes, the journey to show up for someone requires me to walk past the point where I normally stop. Just one step will start the momentum, however, and that's enough. When given the chance and a calorie of forward motion, compassion knows how to outmaneuver complexity.

The best place to start: Mundane moments and small steps. They happen all the time. Although I had to take a big hop to Haiti to figure this out.

The trip began with little fanfare. Our missions team met in the church parking lot, overloaded two vans with suitcases full of first-world stuff to survive a third-world week, drove to the airport, paid excessive weight baggage fees, and boarded a jet that touched down in Port-Au-Prince after several hours. While in Haiti, we assisted tradesmen rebuilding homes an earthquake had torn down, ignored the chemical-warfare-like odor emanating from burning trash, and prayed for wind. We also visited an orphanage for several hours.

A week later, we returned home—but a part of me stayed in Haiti after someone ambushed my heart. No, I didn't meet God in anything to do with the earthquake's damage. No, he didn't seem to appear in any smelly fires. And he certainly had no presence in the wind, or lack thereof. Instead, an unexpected sacred moment came in an unusually quiet and unspectacular fashion. It took place at the orphanage when I met a Haitian boy no older than three.

Without a doubt, the American team brought joy to the orphanage. Partially from the beachballs and bottles of bubbles, partially from the small candy packs, but mostly from our group's high spirits, the result of a day spent away from the construction site. Playing with kids beats pouring cement. Especially when Starburst fruit chews fuel the fun. Many homes in Haiti have tall security walls, which tightly packed all the games and laughs and bubbles into a safe, loud, chaotic area.

Despite the appeal of revelry, one little boy drifted off to sit alone, under a tree against the wall. The truth is that people who most need someone to show up for them very often appear a step or two away from all the action.

I barely noticed him as I chased a ball kicked out of a lively scrum that bopped and booted anything inflated and brightly colored. A shallow drainage ditch separated the quiet plot of shade he occupied and the rest of the compound. Maybe it was curiosity caused by his tears; maybe it was a divine nudge. Who knows—but I rolled the ball toward the crowd, turned away from them, and made a long stride across the trench to sit down next to the little guy.

The only Haitian-Creole words I know include my name, age, and how to ask for the nearest bathroom. He was only three and rightfully knew no English. Good news: to show up for someone doesn't require clever words. Or sometimes, any words at all. Silence is so under-appreciated and under utilized.

With all the fun going on all around him, why did he feel so sad? No easy answer came to mind. So I thought about his life. This beautiful little fella arrived in the world like everybody else, but his life took a very different turn. To live in an orphanage means he spends every day with a lot of people but doesn't have parents. He has to compete for attention, and the competition looks stiff. Real young, real small—he's probably overlooked a lot. From watching how the kids interact with one another, he definitely experiences a lot of injustice within these walls; in games, in meals, and in life overall. With nothing to call his own, he finally has a fun-looking beachball kicked his way, only to have someone take it right away. Countless scrapes, putdowns, and pushes out of the way. This is not the way life is supposed to work. No mom to hold him. No dad to defend him. No one to rely on. No wonder he was sad.

His life brought tears to my eyes, too, so I scooched closer. There we sat, under a tree and against a wall next to a ditch full of stagnant grey water, tears streaming down our faces. Unable to communicate but clearly able to connect at a level deeper than any conversation could ever flow.

With eyes fixed on the drainage swill, his hand grabbed hold of my little finger and squeezed. Not the grip of someone trying to inflict pain. Rather, the clutch of some-one sharing pain and not wanting to let go of the one person who noticed. Eventually, maybe four or five minutes later, he popped up and before I could even shift my weight to stand, he let go of my finger and wrapped both arms around my neck. Definitely the best hug I've ever received.

He took a half step back, and as we both wiped tears off our cheeks, a grin appeared and his eyes went bright—as if a window shade abruptly rolled open to reveal full sunshine. As quick as a bullet, he ran toward the crowd and the chaos, reloaded for fun.

It's easy to watch people from a safe distance. It's easy to fear speaking the wrong words or feel too busy. It's easy to do little or nothing, or to stay safely within the walls of what's familiar and comfortable. The people held down by loneliness rarely lift up their voices to ask for help. If we wait until asked to show up for someone, the wait will run long. In most cases, such a request will never happen. It's hard to make a personal difference from a distance—even when the separation measures only a few steps.

Money will not fill the gap. The orphanage receives strong financial support. They possess plenty of toys, food, and a sturdy structure. But all that made no difference in the moment with my little friend. His was a more basic need, felt by more people than you and I can comprehend. What he needed most is something everyone can do: anyone can care enough to sit down and stay a moment. Even me.

Was the direction of his life altered that day? Nope. That's not the point of this story. In the process of an act as ridiculously simple as a shared moment of time and attention and reaction to his life, my little friend opened *my* eyes to what the world needs most—people willing to show up for one another. No process to follow. No expectations. Not even effort to fix the situation. Just meet him where he's at regardless of where I've come from.

Will he remember me? I don't know, and that's good. To step out of my life story and into someone else's presents a worthy challenge. Instead of playing a lead role, I must feel content with a cameo appearance for one episode. If invited back for a whole season, then I can savor an unexpected honor.

Loneliness is a hole people find themselves in, for whatever the reason. Sometimes for just a moment; other times for a few months, maybe longer. After attempts to stretch, climb, jump, and other futile efforts, exhaustion eventually sets in and they sit down. I've been that person enough to know the only solution: someone willing to show up and extend a hand—or even just a pinky.

Do unto others as you would have done to you.

CHAPTER 2

THINGS HAPPEN FOR A REASON

Lou and I met due to a cancellation.

For months our church had planned a community serving day, during which a small volunteer army would storm the city to perform prearranged odd jobs for people who need assistance. While the tasks would vary in degrees of difficulty—raking leaves to repairing roofs—coordinating all the efforts promised to provide a challenge. So the church relied on an expert in organizing people: my wife Becky. In turn, she relied on me to fill in for volunteers who cancel at the last minute.

So on a cold, grey November Saturday morning, Becky answered a call from someone unable to work. Maybe it was the chilly air. Or the sporadic snowflakes, the first of the season. Or maybe the guy had a legitimate reason. That makes no difference now; I'm glad he backed out. Although in the moment, a few grumpy thoughts came to mind when Becky assigned me leaf raking duty. *C'mon, someone wants a cleaner yard for the snow to cover?*

Wisdom trumped instinct, and I uncharacteristically said nothing as I packed everything needed to gather leaves: rake, tarp, blower, extension cord, gloves, and coffee.

The final challenge to my just-serve-with-a-smile-and-no-sarcasm attitude arrived when Becky shared a comment from the Council on Aging representative who sent in the request to rake an elderly man's yard. "Supposedly he's a real mean, grumpy old guy," she said while handing me the address.

"Have fun."

I tapped the address into my smartphone and drove the eight minutes quoted in the directions to the old guy's house. (The maps crammed into my glove compartment have gone unused for years. I'm not sure I know how to read them anymore, or if I ever should have tried. If texting while driving is dangerous and now illegal, did the authorities just not notice the distraction posed by unfolding a map and trying to follow it while steering with a knee?)

Matt, another volunteer, and I arrived precisely at 9 a.m. We parked in the driveway that extended from the side of the house to the street. The closed garage door made me wonder if anyone was home. "I think I met this guy once," Matt said while we unloaded the cars. "He's pretty gruff."

Along with paper maps, I'm barely familiar with the word "gruff," but imagined it was no compliment. Is he mad, mean, or deranged? Will he yell at us to leave? After all, the wind had blown nearly every leaf out of his yard. Now that we'd seen the matted, leafless grass sugarcoated by shiny snowflakes, we knocked on Lou Marist's door to introduce ourselves. Gotta love community ministry.

After three tries, we stopped knocking and started raking the frozen ground. Close to the house and shrubs, our rakes grabbed hold of more leaves than snow. Funny how a dozen crinkly leaves can make you feel useful. But such a feeling belied reality; this yard needed raking as much as a bald man needs a comb. *Why is it okay to give a volunteer such a lame assignment? I should have insisted on a different project. I know the coordinator real well, or so I thought.* At that very moment, as narcissism began to shut down my heart, the garage door opened—and so did the possibility that this serving opportunity was really not about me.

Matt and I walked toward the garage together, surprised that someone was home. Standing barefoot in his garage leaning on a cane while wearing a white undershirt and faded black slacks, Mr. Marist gave us a bewildered, what-are-you-doing-here look. But his expression completely contradicted his words: "Thank you guys. The yard sure needs raking."

To avoid lying—or laughing—Matt and I said nothing.

"Sorry it took me so long to get out of my back room. Want me to make you some eggs?" Mr. Marist asked.

"No thank you, sir," Matt replied.

"We'll just keep working on your yard, if that's okay," I said.

"Go right ahead," he said, "I'll be right inside here."

As he began to slowly turn around, I noticed his feet moved only a couple inches at a time, and never fully left the cold garage floor. How would he handle the two steps into his house with such a labored shuffle?

"Let me give you a hand with those steps," I said, quickly moving ahead of him to hold the door open, extending my other arm toward him to lean on.

"Thank you, this helps a lot," he said as he labored to lift and plant one foot, then the other.

Matt and I continued our work, filled with new energy and intent. Enthusiasm, however, doesn't create leaves. Twenty minutes later, we had raked everything not connected to the ground—including a few swipes into neighbors' yards to build our anemic leaf volume. We spread out a small tarp that easily swallowed all our work. Plans called for a different volunteer team to come by in a warm, heated truck, set their hot coffees in drink holders, and throw tarps full of leaves into the truck bed. (Yes, all the volunteers showed up for truck duty.)

I thawed my fingers and called the team to let them know they need not stop at Mr. Marist's; we could fit the scantily filled tarp in the back of my vehicle. Possibly even in the glove compartment—after removing the maps, of course.

"Before we leave, let's go tell the old man we're done," I said to Matt. "He didn't seem grumpy (I should've said "gruff"). I think he wanted to talk. This will only take a minute or two."

We knocked on the door and Mr. Marist invited us inside. For the next fifteen minutes, as my eyes wandered around his kitchen and living room, he talked about all the leaves, his house, the neighborhood, serving in World War II, and a host of other general topics that caused my mind to wander.

Then a quick, very matter-of-fact comment yanked my attention back to our host: "My wife died three years ago, so I spend every day sitting alone in my house waiting to die."

One of us abruptly changed the topic and asked him to tell more about the war. His experience as a B-24 tail gunner in the South Pacific seemed much more upbeat and interesting to hear about than a spouse's death.

After declining another offer of eggs and coffee, but accepting the old guy's appreciation, Matt and I left Mr. Marist.

But he stayed with me.

Lou and I met again by divine appointment.

During the Sunday service following our church's community serving day, Pastor Steve crowdsourced his message time by asking for stories from volunteers. Several individuals eager for their turn at the Sunday morning mic gave descriptions of what they did and who they helped. The leaf truck team chuckled about something that happened as they ate breakfast together. I didn't laugh. I also didn't come close to raising my hand to describe scraping up less than two pounds of leaves off a frozen yard.

Embarrassment about the assignment aside, a thought kept coming to mind. In fact a brief debate took place between me and the One who, I believe, insisted on my wrestling with the thought. The internal struggle became so real that all the wonderful stories shared by others turned into white noise, similar to the sound of traffic on the highway bordering the church property. As clear as when I first heard them a day prior, I kept rerunning Mr. Marist's words: "My wife died three years ago, so I spend every day sitting alone in my house waiting to die."

I wanted to rid myself of that memory, but it refused to leave. Over and over his statement, in his voice, replayed. *So what?* I callously thought.

Mr. Marist's words momentarily stopped, and a deeper question filled my mind and penetrated my heart. A question that now sounds smugly noble, but at the time hurt to hear. Is that the way life is supposed to be? Sitting alone waiting to die; is that the way it's supposed to be?

What an easy answer: *no*.

And what a beautiful setup to the next question.

Then what are you going to do about it?

Answer: *I'm not sure.*

But I did know, for certain, that sitting in church was not the right answer. Would God really encourage someone to leave church? No, but only if attending church is the make-or-break point to faith. Yes, on the other hand, if the point of attending church is to relate to, hear from, and respond to God.

So I left. No one noticed. It's amazing how much happens in life that escapes notice. And how many people escape notice too: folks in church—or at home alone. More people really should consider leaving church.

With no specific plan in mind, I found my car and started the engine. Fortunately, my wife staffed the information table that day, so we both had driven—and she hadn't noticed my departure either. Double fortune happened when I opened the map app on my smartphone and it still showed the exact location of Mr. Marist's house. The suggested route took me past a Walmart, and a plan came to mind. Actually, a weak idea. But it was something; it was action to take.

Five minutes later, I placed a fresh loaf of Vienna bread from the bakery next to me on the car seat, and a little voice told me to turn right out of the parking lot. (The voice came from the map app; God had told me all He was going to say back at church.)

Exactly six minutes later, I arrived at the destination. The closed garage door meant nothing; he was likely there because he sits at home all day, alone, waiting to die. So what do I say? That part of the plan remained unclear and unknown on the walk from the driveway to the front door.

I rang the doorbell and waited, nervously passing the bag of Vienna bread from right hand to left and back again, wondering which hand should hold the bread. "Shake with the right and receive with the left." Not exactly the same situation as high school graduation, but that advice does come in handy. What should I say? I rang again, then went on my tiptoes, peering through the transom to see Mr. Marist's white hair as he shuffled to the door.

He opened the door and once again had a bewildered, what-are-you-doing-here look. Before he could say anything I blurted out: "Hi Mr. Marist, I'm David. I raked your yard yesterday, was at the store today, and picked up a loaf of bread for you, if you want one."

I extended the bag for him to see. With my left hand, of course.

To my relief he said, "C'mon in. How did you know I needed bread?"

"A lucky guess," I said, avoiding the nosy truth that I scanned his place while we talked the day before and had noticed a nearly empty loaf bag.

For the next hour, we sat and talked. Actually, I mostly listened, continuing to wonder what I was doing there. But it felt good. It felt right. No one should sit home alone waiting to die. There's nothing I can do to prevent the latter, but I can do something about the alone part. I can show up. Clearly, the old guy deeply enjoyed a person willing to listen and show interest in him. Doesn't everyone share that desire—to know someone else cares, even just a little and for just a moment?

An hour flew past and the time to leave arrived. As I stood, I asked if it was okay for me to return each week to hear more stories.

"Sure it is," he said. "You know where to find me. I don't go anywhere.

"Still can't believe you knew what I needed."

Man shall not live on bread alone.

CHAPTER 3

COMINGS AND GOINGS

Relationships grow when you stick with them long enough to experience the unexpected.

A routine developed for my visits with Mr. Marist. Each week's journey began with a short drive to a restaurant to purchase two small coffees and apple pie slices, then ended with the remaining five-minute trip to his house. Finally, I'd park the car and face an equilibrium challenge; step out while balancing one cup on top of the other and holding the bag of pie, walk from the driveway to the front door, and ring the doorbell with a slow motion elbow tap. Without dropping anything.

And then wait. I'd like to say "patiently," but that would be a lie.

As I stood there an unusually long time (approximately a whopping sixty seconds) on my fourth visit, I began to wonder: *How many people have come to his house and left before he could shuffle over to answer the door?* That very thing had happened the day Matt and I raked his yard. How easy for people filled with noble intentions to show up and serve, only to have such goodwill go bad because something just takes too long. Our quick response/quick results culture encourages an expectation of immediacy. *Or am I trying to blame society for my own junk?*

The true sentiment now hijacking my heart: *C'mon already, I make the effort. I buy the coffee and pie. I drive here. I know you're home alone and not doing anything, so why don't you come to the door faster?*

Finally, the sound of the door chain swinging and deadbolt turning interrupts my self-absorption session. Soon, this immature little fit going on inside me, this I-focused desire to have life happen at my speed and on my terms, will wash away thanks to the coffee and pie.

I stepped through the open doorway to a shocking sight. Mr. Marist stood behind his walker, wearing only his usual pair of black trousers, belt unfastened, no shoes or socks. I nearly dropped the coffee—such was the jolt from seeing a half-naked ninety-one year old man.

Are we seriously that comfortable with one another already? I thought but wisely did not say. With admirable casualness he said, "You caught me trying to wash up for the day. Why don't you call me before coming over here so I can get ready?"

A reasonable request. Actually a common courtesy I expect from and typically extend to others. *Is it possible to take back all those pathetic thoughts while waiting at the door?* Without any mention of attire, or lack thereof, we sat and talked over forkfuls of pie and hot coffee sips.

About a half cup into the conversation, he made another request. "Stop calling me Mr. Marist and call me Lou."

"Okay, Lou," I said.

"Growing up, I was called Weasel," he said. "Because even though I was small, I was tough as hell. People learned not to mess with the Weasel."

Sitting there half-clothed, Lou did not look like a weasel. But I took him at his word.

"So is it okay for me to call you Weasel?"

"Sure. I kinda like hearing someone call me that. You'll be the only one, though."

"Why? Doesn't anyone else know that was your nickname?"

"No one who ever called me Weasel is still alive."

"Maybe I'll just stick with Lou."

Simple questions. Simple answers. Good conversation. Good coffee and pie. And now, the welcome arrival of informality—a clear sign of a growing relationship.

The next week I honored Lou's request and called to ask if I could visit. Although I told him I'd be there in twenty minutes, delays in leaving and an unusually long wait to buy coffee and pie resulted in a half-hour delay. As I turned off Mercury Drive onto the street where Lou lives, an unexpected and unforgettable sight pierced my insensitivity toward my tardiness. Tremendous lessons typically happen in unplanned moments. And such an instant arrived.

At the end of his undisturbed, snow-covered driveway his garage door stood open. And there stood Lou, fully clothed, in the entry between the house and the garage, looking toward the road. *He opened the garage door because I'm coming over,* I realized. *And he's been standing there waiting for me this whole time.*

There is no better feeling than feeling welcome.

Without giving up he stood, aided by a walker, and waited an extra half hour—a full twenty-nine minutes longer than my frustration point on his front porch a week earlier. It's amazing how people will patiently wait because they value a person willing to show up for them.

Since that visit, I call ahead; I tell him when to expect me, and I make sure to arrive on time. The remainder of our routine remains the same: visit the restaurant, wonder why I do this as I drive to Lou's house, whine to myself about the time it takes and the other things I could be doing, and then have my heart burst with joy when I round the corner and see the open garage door. Just for me. *Remind me, please, who's serving whom?*

Ah, the power of mutuality. When two people feel served by one another, a hearty relationship sprouts and grows.

Admittedly, the shorter walk from the car through the open garage and into the house is much easier to navigate while balancing the coffee and pie. In fact, Lou just yells, "Come" when I tap the door with my foot. Yes, we feel quite comfortable with one another.

My familiarity with his home eventually expanded to well beyond his garage and front room. In fact, a visit to his basement was particularly memorable, in a manner similar to near-crashes on highways.

Just a few steps into our descent, I wondered if this was a good idea. Our journey went slow. With cane hooked over his forearm, Lou slid one foot until it dropped down to the next stair, then repeated with the other foot. It sounded rhythmic, almost dramatic. Swish, plop, swish, plop. The unusually steep and narrow staircase, illuminated by a single bare light bulb fifty watts too dim, made eerie sounds too. The slow creak with every step made me wonder about the construction quality, the catastrophic consequences of termite damage, or if a Stephen King movie scene awaited.

What will we find down there? Or, what will find us? Turning around was not an option.

Once we safely landed, Lou proudly pointed out architectural aspects of the walls, wiring, and room width. He tapped his cane on the ceiling and asked if I noticed the height. No, I hadn't because my eyes continually scanned the room for suspicious movements from anything or anyone that might lie in wait just around the corner. The damp, thick air tasted stale, as though it had remained stagnant for years. I glanced at my cell phone to make sure it still held a strong signal—just in case.

The tour lasted only a few minutes, and included a shuffle through the workshop filled with sharp tools capable of who-knows-what in the wrong hands. Finally, we stood at the bottom of the stairs to face a new and equally scary challenge; the ascent. Fully aware that gravity would work against Lou if he took a tumble, I suggested he go first. As we reached the halfway point he said, "Are you behind me to catch me if I start to fall?"

"That's right," I said.

"Well I hope you're ready."

Before I could ask why, he began tilting backward like a bowling pin falling in slow motion. His warning gave me just enough time to plant my left foot one step higher than my right, and to put both hands in his upper back. An adrenaline-powered moment later, I returned him to his full and upright position.

Together, with his shuffles and my hands propping him, we made it. As we stood in his kitchen, he admitted to feeling out of breath.

"So are you," he observed, "I told you it was a long staircase."

With the excitement of a field trip behind us, we returned to our normal routine. I set his coffee and pie in front of him and settled into a chair across the breakfast table. Talking is much easier when we face one another. Nearly on cue from a sitcom script, he says, "You bring this because you think my coffee is lousy."

"That's right."

"You know you don't have to always do this. I don't want you to feel sorry for me."

"Oh, you know I don't. Let's just enjoy being two friends chatting over pie and coffee. There's nothing wrong with that, is there, Weasel?"

And with a grin—worn by us both—the talking begins. I ask about his life. He tells stories. True, he shares the same dozen or so. But he often remembers a new detail each time, so I listen carefully to make sure I catch it. Our times together eventually conclude in equally predictable fashion.

"Lou, it's time for me to go. I'll give you a call before I come to see you next weekend."

"That's fine, you can check to see if I'm still here. I might die first, you know."

"No Lou, I'm planning to be here. So don't die before then. Deal?"

"Okay, deal."

With a solid agreement firmly in place, I step into the garage to leave.

Six months into our friendship, Lou broke our routine by calling out, "David, come back here."

As I walked back inside. He said, "I'm still not sure why you take time every week to come here and visit with me, but I'm glad you do. I appreciate every moment you've been here."

"I enjoy coming here too, Lou."

"I'd like to say that I love you, but that would be a weird thing to say because we're not family."

"How about we say that we share the love of friendship?"

"I'm okay with that. Here, take these two bags of jelly beans. I bought them for you to chew on."

Let love be genuine.

CHAPTER 4

THAT'S WHAT FRIENDS ARE FOR

Life works better together.

Lou enjoys testing the strength of such truths, especially through candid comments that come across as rather acidic: "Honestly, I'm not sure why anyone would want to waste their time on an old man like me."

Some statements are hard to respond to—and best left with no response to avoid a) hurting his feelings or b) sounding pompous. His words provide clues, though, for why loneliness serves as his consistent companion.

Lou fought in World War II and continues to fight with—and through—life, armed with only a slight ration of love and caring that the war doesn't still hold prisoner. Filled with grit and grump, he can be easy for people to dislike or dismiss, and even harder to understand. Come close and he machine guns through memories, pausing only to describe why he's mad about something. Or, at times, everything.

Yet underneath his body armor sits a man whose life deserves dignity and respect. Not for the sum of his decisions and actions; even he readily admits that. There's just something about Lou that makes a person want to give him a reason to smile. Maybe because life doesn't send many reasons his way. Maybe because he's a patriot who willingly fought hard and along the way surrendered the very joy his service preserved for others. Or maybe God really did create all of us to connect with others, so our hearts beat just a little faster when we cross paths with someone like Lou.

A person's loneliness, whatever the cause, is reason enough to reach out to him, to waste time on him (even if he is gritty and grumpy), to make life the way it should be for someone who can only hope for how it could be. "Nobody wants to get to know anyone these days, and that's too bad," says Lou. "Life's full of folks who could be friends."

He shared this with me late on a June Saturday afternoon, and sensing a rare chink in the armor I asked, "Want to go to a graduation party for a friend? It's only two blocks away."

"No, you know I told you I don't like being anywhere when there's a bunch of people."

"I thought you might have changed your mind."

"At 91 you don't change your mind about anything."

Stubborn? Yes! But rewind his life seven decades, and a big reason to extend grace, along with dignity and respect, comes into sight. As the tail gunner in a B-24 bomber who completed 40 missions in the South Pacific, planes shot bullets straight at Lou as he fired his weapon at them—an ongoing nightmare that he faced with eyes wide open. In doing so, certain images permanently burned into his long-term memory and, as a result, shaped his life view. Especially with respect to relationships.

"I remember spending many nights playing cards, talking about what we were going to do back home. And the next day we'd fly for hours in formation. Then Jap [Japanese] fighters or ack-ack [anti-aircraft fire] would show up, and all hell would break loose. But we'd stay in formation; you knew the guys in the bombers on both sides of you. Eventually, someone would take a hit. It's something to see friends blown out of the sky. Something you never forget. That happened with too many guys I knew."

Some statements are hard to respond to and perhaps best left with no response.

"The Army told us to never get close with anyone because that would happen. But how do you not get to know people? And when you get to know 'em, you can't help but consider 'em friends."

Travel back far enough with someone, and who that person is and why he is that way come into focus. To take that journey, though, requires time and patience, perhaps hearing stories for ten (or more) times, and the willingness to ignore grumpiness. Along with an appetite for coffee and pie. The effort to know 'em—really know 'em—pays off in life's ultimate reward: a friendship. A treasure with a lifespan not counted in years.

"Those guys, my friends, are gone, but they never really leave me."

Apparently, the same truth holds for enemies. Late in the war, enemy fighter pilots began to fly their planes like guided missiles into American bombers. Lou recalls a close call with one such attempt during a mission when several U.S. planes went down.

"Our crew said we had a fighter coming straight at us. From my position in the tail, I couldn't see him until he banked hard up and to the right. None of us know why he didn't ram us, but he didn't. So I opened up on him with my guns. He flew so close to us that I could see the pilot as clear as I see you. He smiled at me and had big, gold teeth. I still have dreams at night about that smile and those teeth.

"I wasn't sure if I knocked him out or not. But the next day, Tokyo Rose said on the radio that they got a few of our bombers and only lost one fighter. Nobody else claimed a hit, so I think I got ole 'Gold Teeth.'

"Why did he pull out at the last moment? I'll never know. But I do feel like I owe him my life for doing it. That smile of his makes me think he was a bit crazy."

Maybe war does that to people. The story that Lou tells, retells, and tells again, more than any other story, involves a friend he made while stationed at the airbase on Morotai, a south Pacific island.

Airmen constantly arrived to start a fresh tour of duty and relieve those who had completed their forty-six combat mission commitment. Friendships formed, despite the Army's instructions, between those flying in the same aircraft as well as those at similar points in their journey to log forty-six flights. Hit the big "four-six," and your next flight takes you home.

At least that's how the system typically worked.

"I got to know this guy who had served just a little longer than me," Lou said. "He flew as a navigator, so I thought he was pretty smart. Turns out he wasn't. He was crazy.

"I remember a couple days after he hit his forty-six, he volunteered to fly another mission while he waited to catch a flight home. I told him, 'You're nuts! Stay on the ground and wait. You earned it.' But he said he was bored and wanted to fly. Lots of guys did it because they love flying. So up he went. His bomber was next to mine in the formation.

"In the air over our target island, we started taking ack-ack. From the tail, I could look down and see it coming up. Never did like how that looked. One shot looked like it was coming close. It missed us, but hit his bomber. When ack-

ack hits a bomber before it has dropped its load [bombs], there's a big explosion. The crew doesn't have a chance; doesn't even know what happened because it goes so fast.

"He shouldn't have been up there that day. He shouldn't have flown anywhere but home. I should've grabbed him hard, looked him in the eye, and tried like hell to make him stay down. I should've been a better friend.

"A plane came the next day. Brought fresh guys and turned around to go back home. That's the flight my buddy should've been on. A few missions later I hit my forty-six and didn't give a thought to volunteering for another one. Guess he helped me not do something crazy. I owe him that much, 'cause I made it home.

"That was a big surprise because I went into the Army and never expected to come home alive. But now look at us, talking about it seventy years later."

I listen to Lou for hours, but will never truly relate to his war experience. Yet I can remember a season of life when I, too, wondered whether I would make it out alive.

At age thirty-six, I changed careers and began full time work on a church staff. The team was large, and we had a constant flow of people coming and going. The first friends I made were with others on the management team, especially Robyn who started working there about the same time as I did.

At thirty-seven I had cancer. The diagnosis came so fast and seemingly from nowhere that it was hard to know what happened. Especially when the odds of surviving five more years stood at 50-50. That information helped make the decision easy to try an experimental treatment following surgery. After all, I wanted to hit my own forty-six—and many more.

The protocol involved extremely high doses of a drug five days a week for a month. Living just ten minutes away from a chemotherapy clinic offered the option to stay home and take a daily commute to therapy. The church management team put together a transportation rotation schedule so my wife wouldn't have to drive every day.

Each treatment lasted three hours. At first, I tolerated the drug well. Soon, though, in the short time elapsed after removing the intravenous line from my arm and leaving the clinic, a downward spiral would begin. The greatest hope was to tough it out, make it home fast, and sleep away the sickness. But the time it took for the effects to show up kept growing shorter. And I didn't stay tough.

Robyn's first rotation came early in week two. She sat in an adjacent chair to chat while the drugs dripped into my arm and began their mission. When the solution bags went empty, the nurses put a Band-Aid on my arm and took my vital signs once more before we headed out the door.

All seemed quite routine until we stepped into the bright afternoon sunshine. Robyn had parked in one of the few spots remaining that morning, on the parking lot's back row.

She continued chatting while we walked, working hard to keep my spirits up. Rather than take the long route via the sidewalk along the outside of the lot, we walked straight through the parked cars. Usually it's a very uneventful adventure, unless a person had just received an extremely high dose of a cancer-fighting drug.

Exactly where it happened, I can't recall. But at some point, I felt disoriented and slowed my walking. Robyn, still chatting, kept going. Upon approaching another row of cars, I couldn't see her—or even hear her. I had no idea where I was. All I could see were cars everywhere. I panicked. I was lost. I stopped behind a car's back bumper, and there I stood. Alone. Shaking.

Soon, Robyn came back to find me.

"There you are."

As she approached, I swallowed my just-need-to-tough-it-out pride and said, "I don't know where I am. Please help me. I can't do this on my own."

Fortunately, Robyn and I must have built a strong enough friendship over the year and a half we had worked together because she looked me in the eye and through her big smile assured me all would be well.

"Oh, c'mon," she said. "It's no big deal. We're almost there."

Then she took hold of my trembling hand and steered me to her car. She continued talking the whole way, working hard to keep my spirits up.

I made it home that day.

To my knowledge, Robyn never mentioned that episode to anyone—although she did tell the other drivers to make sure they parked close to the building.

Sometimes what's needed most in life is a friend to show up and just grab your hand. Not to fix you or judge you; just to help you find your way. For a short walk or a long season. Early in life, in the middle, or as the finish line approaches.

"David, if my time comes before you come back here next week, promise me you won't get too upset with me," Lou said.

"Lou, when your time comes, you can go knowing that you and I stayed friends until the very end," I replied. "There's nothing for either of us to be upset about."

"Looks like we've got a deal, friend."

Some statements are so rich, so life-giving, and so heartfelt that they need no response.

It's not good for man to be alone.

CHAPTER 5

REGRETS

In relationships, do whatever you must to avoid regrets.

"Lou, if it were possible to go back in time, what would you change?"

With eyes fixed on the full coffee cup his shaky hand gripped, Lou focused on lifting the cup to his mouth before any splashed out. Experience firing a machine gun out of one moving plane and into another had helped him develop strong hand-eye coordination; he never spilled a drop. The task also gave him time to offer a thoughtful response.

"If I could do my life over, I'd get more education," he said, "and become a doctor."

"But Lou, you never liked to read."

"Oh yeah, guess that would've made it hard. Should've learned to read better. I know I could've been a great doctor, though."

Would've. Should've. Could've. Three common code words that signal regret. Some regrets run deep; some run away and never bother us again. Others seem to hide and take years to resurface.

More than four decades ago I attended third grade Sunday school taught by a retired secretary named Mary, a faithful volunteer at our church where her husband Gordon worked as the custodian. Our family attended every weekend for years, but the most vivid memory of my entire early church experience involves Mary and Gordon and a choice, to my regret, that I wish I "would've" not made.

Mary closely followed the third-grade curriculum workbook lessons, so every week ran just like the week before. Even the Sunday school collection proved predictable; seventy-five cents from our room (half the six-student class remembered to ask their parents for quarters). The total from all the classrooms reliably totaled seventy-five dollars, an amount printed in the church bulletin each Sunday. After noticing this week-after-week consistency, I wondered if that amount would ever change. Did my class's three quarters even matter?

The lone variable in Mary's class monotony came when she asked one lucky student to collect the offering. Eventually, I cracked the code to the selection—she followed the assigned seating chart. (Nine-year olds occupy their minds with such mysteries.) This cherished, break-the-monotony task involved slowly walking past fellow third graders, receiving the three quarters, placing them in a reusable thick blue envelope with our room number on it, and then writing the date and cash total with a very sharp pencil in the tiny, pre-printed grid on the reverse side. The final and critical step involved placing the envelope outside the door for Gordon to collect. The process took place with such routine that Mary paid no attention as she sipped her coffee and scanned the lesson we would soon begin.

Every sixth Sunday my turn arrived, and when it did I had a plan. Instead of writing ".75" on the envelope, I recorded "7.50." My story if caught: a simple mistake with the decimal point. My true intent: hope that Gordon fails to notice so that the published number would finally change. To my delight, the next Sunday's bulletin showed an unusual uptick in the Sunday School offering! (Third graders live for such adventures.)

Sitting in Mary's classroom, I couldn't keep this to myself, so I decided to expand the plan. As I slowly handed a quarter to my buddy Kris, I told him what had happened. His allegiance proved easy to gain; he even took the adventure to the next level and recorded 75.00. Later in the hour, we recruited Todd, who pledged 750.00 when his turn arrived the following week.

For likely the first time ever, third graders at Simpson Church (well, at least three of us) looked forward to Mary's class. I remember dressing in record time that next Sunday morning, impatiently waiting in the car, and finally telling the rest of my family to hurry up so we could arrive earlier than usual.

Unfortunately, the bulletin did not post the Sunday school offering. Odd. When class began, Mary sat down her coffee and collected our quarters. Uh oh. I scanned the lesson we would soon begin, feigning interest in an attempt to avoid eye contact as I handed her my coin. She personally handled and recorded the money every week thereafter. Todd, who sat closest to the door, reported that a different person now gathered the envelopes. The three of us never received a reprimand. Clearly, Gordon did.

Over forty years have passed since the great collection caper. Along the way, I have served on a church staff and gained appreciation for the importance of handling money well—and the need to take appropriate steps if suspicions arise. Yes, I feel genuinely sorry for lying about the amount. My largest regret focuses on what the mischief likely did to Gordon—and that I put off stepping forward to apologize for so long that I forgot about the incident. Gordon likely never did. I wronged a good man.

Everyone makes mistakes. Regret, though, often sets in from not stepping forward or not showing up to say the words that would've, could've, or should've changed everything. For people we know well. For people we barely know. Even for people we don't know at all, but need the words we can share. The window of opportunity for speaking up can close and, it seems, become boarded over.

"I wish I hadn't accumulated so many regrets," Lou remarked. "Never knew I had so many of 'em till I got old."

The most painful regrets involve relationships. "I visited my sister last weekend," Lou said. "Lots of people were there to see her. I think she knew they were there because she wasn't going to make it much longer. Why do people wait until it's almost too late to show up?

"I gave her $100 and told her to go shopping. She always liked to shop, so I wanted her to do it again. For once, I wanted to give her a reason to be happy. She and I talked on the phone the next day and she said she was excited to go shopping soon. But she never made it out before we lost her."

"Lou, what a nice thing to do for her," I said.

"Didn't you hear me? She died. She never went shopping."

"But it was still nice."

"Yeah, but it was too late. I should've given her the money a long time ago."

Yes, timing is everything. The longer we wait to take action, the more we invite regret. And although anyone can enjoy a relationship when times are warm and well, when a deep chill arrives, we need to show up by doing or saying something unexpected to break the ice. Even small steps can result in major progress.

Amy and I live in the same town, where we met at a parenting workshop. Even though I served as the speaker that evening, it is the story she told me that I'll always remember best. Amy and her husband had disagreed with their son's decision to drop out of college and start a job fifteen hours away. Just four classes stood between him and a walk across the stage to receive his degree. Instead, he wanted to relocate halfway across the country.

Occasional conversations about his plans always ended with harsh words; the type that dig an ever-widening gap between people. He refused to listen to his parents' counsel. Everyone cramped with frustration and tried to avoid the issue.

With talking no longer an option, and in an effort to relieve some of the maddening pressure building inside her, Amy woke up early one morning and decided to write about her feelings.

She understood that relational issues often become the plaque that blocks an artery—an unwanted obstacle that prevents the flow of life-giving love. This mom wanted to feel the love again.

On a blank card, she wrote the many reasons she believed in her son, why she treasured him, and described how he could count on her no matter what. Heartfelt statements, but effective only if delivered well and at just the right time. Unsure of when that time would come, Amy slid the note into an envelope with her son's name on it. As she finished her coffee and looked at the envelope, she let out a big sigh. *Maybe tonight when I come home from work,* she thought, while grabbing her keys to leave for the day.

"Mom, wait!" her son yelled, running barefoot toward her car as she backed down their long driveway.

She stopped and rolled down her window. Before she could say a word he said, "Get out of the car right now!"

Concerned that something was terribly wrong, she opened her door and stepped out. Actually, something was wonderfully right. Yes, timing is everything.

He wrapped his arms around her while still holding the note he had found, opened, and read while pouring his own coffee. "I'm so glad you still believe in me," he told her as their embrace continued longer than any had for many years.

The time is always right for words that will repair a relationship and, along the way, avoid future regret. When the urge arrives, take action. Although in some cases, a person can earn relational hero status by what's *not* said. For that reason, give Lou a medal.

The day of the week often proves challenging for Lou to recall, but details surrounding missions seventy years ago fly out of him with ease. At points during his stories his eyes seem to focus on the action as it takes place, and his voice strengthens. For extended moments, Lou journeys back to the South Pacific.

"We went on a mission over Cebu City [Philippines] to drop a load of thousand-pound bombs. Our plane flew in the back of the formation, with another group following us.

"From the tail, I watched those same planes for hours. Gets pretty boring until you reach the target—or fighters come after you. Over Cebu City the ack-ack was thick, so explosions were popping all over the place. I could see ack-ack rise up from the ground and watch it explode between planes.

"We dropped our load, and I still didn't have anything to fire at so I watched the formation behind us drop theirs. One of the planes must have drifted because I saw a thousand-pounder drop right into the middle of it. Those bombs aren't supposed to detonate until they hit the ground, but this one did. One moment there was a bomber, the next minute a giant flash. Then the whole thing was just gone. I'm guessing the bomb that hit it set off their entire load.

"When other planes were hit, I'd watch for guys jumping out and count them. On this one, there was nothing to jump out of—it just went 'poof' and was gone. I saw the whole thing happen."

As Lou described the explosion's intensity, his eyes opened wide and lit up like small balls of flame—as if he was inside the B-24 and watching the whole tragedy happen again.

"Back at the base, the bombardiers from two planes found me and asked me which one of them dropped the bomb that hit the plane. Both were in position to do it, and neither of them would've seen which one did it. They figured I was in the tail and was the only person who could've seen. And they were right. I knew which one dropped the bomb."

As he finished his story, Lou turned his sights from the window he stared out and looked directly at me. He was back in Michigan and ready to take another shaky sip of coffee, but not quite finished with the story.

"I didn't want one of them to live with a horrible regret, so I told them I didn't see. What good would've come from saying anything? I never told them, and I'm not even going to tell you. We were in that war together; that's how we made it."

A friend loves at all times.

CHAPTER 6

FERTILIZER, WATER, AND THE NEED TO BE CLOSE

The best way to reach someone is from the shortest possible distance.

Before we started eating pie one sunny April Saturday afternoon, the doorbell chimed. Lou showed no reaction. When it rang again, I offered to answer the door. "Go ahead," he said, "but I'm not buying anything."

On the front stoop stood a young woman in her late teens or early twenties, wearing a neon green t-shirt from a local landscaping company. Her glowing smile communicated three messages: 1) surprise that someone opened the door and smiled back, 2) youthful exuberance, likely to discourage anyone from asking for her solicitor's permit, and 3) innocence that initiated immediate trust—or at least suspended suspicion.

She said her name, company, and details of the lawn services available in a tight and well-rehearsed 30-second spurt that required no pause for breath and offered no hope for interruption. After finishing with a smile, she didn't hesitate at the invitation to step inside and meet the owner of the house. After all, it's hard to shout a refined sales pitch from far away. A quick mental note came to mind: *Never let my daughter work for any company that would allow her to eagerly walk into strangers' houses.*

To this young salesperson's credit, she maintained her big smile as Lou shuffled toward her wearing his who-are-you-and-what-do-you-want expression. For a guy who claims to see and hear poorly, he noticed her about to start talking and beat her to the first complete word. He acknowledged the need for someone to fertilize, but only if that person gave his yard the right treatment.

He went on to describe how a previous lawn service applied weed killer that also wiped out most of his grass: "They never came out here to see what they did, and they kept dumping the same stuff on my yard that they dump on everyone else's. Some guy on a computer just sat on his ass and decided what I needed without ever looking at my yard. He didn't help it, he ruined it. How does your company work?"

In lawns and in lives it's hard to make a positive, lasting difference from a distance.

Her bright smile had substantially dimmed by this point. Maybe because Lou took at least ten minutes to describe, redescribe, and describe once more his displeasure with last year's lawn service. Maybe her face muscles grew tired. Or maybe she knew what she was about to ask.

"If you sign this box, our representative will call you and schedule your first treatment," she said, forcing the smile to return. I winced at the thought of what Lou might say next if he fully understood what she had just told him.

"Go ahead and have them call me. I'm not signing anything until someone looks at my yard. When will someone be here?"

"I don't know. But if you sign this box, someone will call you and give you a quote."

"But how will they know what to do?"

They exchanged multiple volleys, neither backing off their positions. So I offered a compromise: I signed the box so the energetic representative would receive credit from her company for securing a lead and Lou would avoid any commitment.

A week later, Lou couldn't remember if the company had called. He felt completely sure, though, that no one had looked at his yard. After he described (in repetitive detail) last years' experience with the impersonal lawn service orchestrated by a man at a distant computer terminal, I offered a new solution to feed his starving yard. "I fertilize my yard, so I'll buy extra and do your yard this week too."

"I don't like owing anybody anything," Lou said. "So I'll give you money to buy the fertilizer. How much do you want for putting it on?"

"You can pay for the fertilizer, but I'm not taking any money for doing it."

"Of course I'm paying for the fertilizer. But how much do I pay *you*?"

The battle of the wills bounced back and forth a few times and eventually landed on the free labor approach.

We talked at length about lawn care that day. His face blossomed with a big smile when he heard about my longtime wish for a well to water my yard. According to Lou, he's one of only a few people in the world gifted at finding the optimum location to drive a well. It's called water witching, water dowsing, or rhabdomancy. His description of how this unusual talent works aligns well with the unique name: He holds a common, long handsaw by the blade end. When he walks over a spot above a deep stream of running water, the saw begins to wobble. Count the times the blade goes up and down, and that's how many feet deep to drill.

Yeah, right.

"So here's the deal," Lou said. "You fertilize my yard, and I'll witch yours to find water."

While preferring to decline his offer and just help him without recompense, another thought sprang to mind: There's dignity in reciprocation. Whether the value of the exchange proves equal doesn't matter. A one-way relationship is, after all, no relationship. Somewhat akin to the grass-killing man behind the computer at the lawn service headquarters.

Give Lou credit for consistency.

Three evenings later, I called to tell Lou he could expect me soon. He sat outside on his walker and waited for me. Following his brief inspection of the fertilizer bag and a short interrogation about the product quality (requiring my multiple promises to not kill his yard), I told him it would take a half hour to apply. Thirty minutes later Lou asked when he could witch my yard. No negotiation needed; we agreed on Saturday. But he wasn't quite through with this visit.

"I know you think witching is b.s.," he said, "so let me show you right now. Go get my saw."

Maybe he *can* find water because he absolutely can read a mind.

Lou shuffled behind his walker to a spot in his yard where years ago he had found water and drove a well.

Decades later, there was still plenty of water—a true water witch success story. He asked again for me to fetch a saw hanging on a hook in his garage. The darkened, worn-wood handle and rusty blade matched Lou well; it looked like his saw. Probably a trusty tool dating back to when he built the house. And because the house stands strong and straight sixty years later, this saw did what it was created to do quite well.

Cutting lumber and finding water share nothing in common, however.

With one hand on his walker for balance, he held the saw blade end with his other, the weight of the handle causing a big droop. When held over the sidewalk alongside the house, it remained still. Then Lou put the saw over the well top, and it began to quaver. Back to the sidewalk, nothing; over the well, up and down.

Lou counted the motions. At 18, the saw paused. That's when he confirmed that he drove the well 18 feet.

Yea, right.

I wanted to ask if the saw's power caused his wrist and elbow to move too. But what good would that do? This was not my moment to ruin. In fact, another moment quickly arrived that made me glad I had said nothing.

"Let's see if you have the gift," Lou said.

In a smug okay-I'll-play-along attitude, I held the rusty saw blade between my thumb and index finger. It drooped and stayed still, similar to my belief in rhabdomancy. "Guess I don't."

That's when Lou let go of his walker and wrapped both arms around my waist, head tucked into the small of my back. An awkward moment, for sure; we had never touched one another before.

This feels strange. Real strange. But why? How many times have I heard about the power of appropriate physical touch? About the love it shares, the healing it can bring, the need people have for it. Why is this no problem for me with people I care for but feels undeniably uncomfortable now? After all, I know Lou fairly well.

It's because he's old and frail. And his arms barely make it around me. I'm afraid he'll fall. He smells of an old person; like a mix of musty basement air and baby powder. Or a funeral home. In so many ways, he's different. That's it.

That's not it, though. There's something more than the embrace. Lou is doing the hugging here—not me. I show up for him, but on my terms and in ways that I control. Can I show up for someone else, completely give up control, and learn to feel comfortable? Until that happens, I'm holding something back. But the old water witch himself holds back nothing.

Lou asks, "I can't see; is it working?"

That goofy feeling just multiplied! This isn't a friendly, affectionate embrace; he's hoping that the contact between us turns on the saw.

Under my breath, I say a quick apology to Jesus for what I'm about to do. A moment earlier, I felt strange having this old man make contact with me. Now I planned to tell a lie because I wanted to touch his heart and make it dance.

"It's moving, look at it!"

He moves his head a little to the right, still hugging me. Fortunately, he could see the handle move up and down. Equally fortunate, he couldn't see the movement of my wrist. "Yes!" he says with a strong voice and joyful tone I had not heard from him ever before. "I knew this would work. I knew I could give you my energy. How many times did it move?"

"Only twelve or thirteen."

The truth about lies: Although the first one seems hard, it always primes the pump for others to effortlessly flow out.

"That's okay," he says. "You'll get better over time."

Yeah, right.

A few days later we made the short drive to my house. When we arrived, my son Scott stood on one side of Lou to assist as he walked across our yard, saw in hand. No movement anywhere, which meant no water. Strange that at one point, he stood right over the water main leading into my house while a sprinkler ran. Plenty of water rushing through that pipe, yet undetected. Maybe his saw needs recalibrating.

Rhabdomancy can tire out a person. After agreeing to try again another time when he had more energy, we drove back to his house. Scott rode along to add a fresh voice to the conversation. Plus, Lou enjoyed explaining to him how water witching works, or is supposed to work.

Back at his house, Lou found his second wind and decided to give Scott a demonstration. The three of us had plenty of practice moving together as a trio, so we took an entire lap around Lou' house—stopping only for the saw's sporadic movements. When we arrived at his well cap, the saw did its thing. "Let's see if you have the gift," Lou said as he handed the saw to Scott.

The old man showed the young man how to correctly hold the saw. Nothing.

I knew what was coming next.

With Lou wrapped around his waist, Scott and I made eye contact. My son's expression told me that he felt similar angst to what I experienced just a few days earlier. Fortunately, we share an almost Jedi-like gift to read one another's minds without saying a word. I gave Scott a clear head nod, slowly up and down at the speed a water witching saw should move. Then I silently said another quick apology to Jesus.

"Hey, it's starting to move," Scott said with excitement. "Can you see it?"

Funny how a saw's slight wobble could cut through life's ups and downs to release a gusher of delight.

Exhausted from all the walking, witching, and energy sharing, Lou decided to go inside and call it a day. "A wonderful day," he remarked as we departed.

While our yard might be void of water, Scott and I left a man filled with joy. I could argue that, technically, the saw did move so we told Lou the truth. After all, he never asked why the saw moved—so we just didn't say that it was our wrists instead of water.

Okay, we lied to him. Some people will disagree with that decision. I'd do it again. But a larger question looms.

Did Lou give us any gift?

Yes, his embrace gave us a tremendous opportunity. He enabled us to stretch out of personal comfort zones. We received the gift of a chance to fill someone's day with a deep joy not felt (or even detected) for years. That moment interrupted my life. Or at least it tapped a fresh desire to, if given the chance, reach out and extend love to another person. While I want that to be true all the time, it isn't.

Sometimes it takes a bold nudge—or an unexpected hug—to convert my noble intentions into worthy actions. I want more "sometimes" to happen.

Yes, Lou did share something amazing with Scott and me when he wrapped his arms around us.

Love made that saw move.

Love is kind.

CHAPTER 7

SPEAKING OF LOVE

You only miss someone you truly love.

Every time we met, Lou mentioned how much he missed his wife. About three years earlier, after an extended illness and stay in a nursing home, she had passed away. In her place, loneliness became Lou's faithful companion. Old age claimed many corners of his memory but never came close to making him forget Ruth.

With the passion of a man many years younger, he repeated a piece of advice more times than I can count: "David, you make sure to love your wife and never stop. Because one day, one of you will be gone. And it sure gets lonely."

The unaskable question I routinely pondered: *Did he love his spouse as much when she was alive as he does now that she's gone? And did she feel his affection?* After all, sentiment delayed is sentiment denied.

A better question to address: *What about* my *wife—how well do I follow his counsel?*

In mid-December I gave Lou a Christmas card that included my family's picture. For several weeks, the card stood propped up on the counter next to his phone; a place of honor, with no other pictures competing for attention. He probably used the photo as a reminder of my identity when I called before visiting—allowing him time to find and wear a white undershirt. The temperature in his house stayed a toasty 85 degrees, comfortable for short sleeves, bare feet, and the likely reason his rather thick head of white hair partially stood up.

The Saturday following Christmas, Lou gave me reason to chuckle as I stood up to leave. "I know why you haven't brought your wife over here to see me," he said. "'Cause you know I'll give her two looks!"

So on New Year's Day, my wife went with me to visit my elderly friend. I fought hard to suppress laughter when he answered the door wearing his best sweater, dress pants, dress shoes, and neatly combed hair! Lou gave her at least two looks and and his full attention for an hour. He even hugged her goodbye that day. Wait—he's never offered a hug when I leave.

So the question remains: Do I make a big enough fuss over my spouse? After all, I made formal promises that I would. At least twice.

The first commitment took place on our wedding day; a memorable ceremony in front of a big crowd. (Memorable to the bride and groom, at least.) As a 27-year-old, I said my vows and "I dos" with all the conviction a young man can muster. The second promise came in a conversation with, of all people, my father-in-law when I was 45 and much more seasoned by life.

My wife's dad and I shared the same first name, which for many years felt like our only common ground. The rich love he felt for his daughter compelled him to tolerate me. He did it well. My value rose considerably with the arrival of our children, Dave's grandchildren. As fellow dads, our relationship gelled. Two cancer battles, first mine then his, created an even greater common bond. I won mine (so far). Dave is gone.

And I sure miss him.

When the cancer spread to his esophagus, everyone knew the end drew near. Especially Dave. At the time, I worked on a church staff, so he selected me to officiate his funeral service—an event he insisted on arranging. So for six months, I regularly showed up at his house for lengthy planning sessions that included just the two of us. At some point our time together turned a corner, and he began to share his life's every detail. Age failed to claim his memory, so we spent hour upon hour discussing dreams, failures, victories, regrets, relationships, and life perspectives polished to a clarity that comes only by eternity's rapid approach.

While our relationship began with distance years earlier, we became tight in those concluding months. What a treasure it was to share love while he was still alive.

In what would be our final time together, Dave looked over his bent and torn yellow legal pad on which he made notes about the service and to-do items. Most lines contained names of people we agreed he needed to meet with and say something to before he departed. He updated me on the last of those meetings. We discussed how to work the Purdue University fight song into his funeral service, and he set down his pen. "Looks like we did it all," he said, signaling that we had reached our planning marathon's finish line.

"No, there's one more thing," I replied.

"The service is done, and I did everything we talked about," Dave said.

"Well, it's something I want you to know as the final thing we talk about," I said. We both knew the inevitable would happen soon.

I took a deep breath and said, "I promise to love your daughter well—and to never stop."

A long, quiet, holy moment later, during our unusually lengthy hug farewell, he whispered, "I know you will."

The day I started writing this book began with a walk to the end of our town's long pier that extends into Lake Michigan. The gusty winds created big waves that rhythmically pounded the pier's cement walls. Watching the water's massive peaks and troughs has a hypnotic effect, broken only when unusually strong waves hit the cement with the right force and angle to send walls of water spraying high into the air. Ironically, witnessing this display of natural brute force results in a peaceful feeling—likely from feeling so small.

As I sat on a cement ledge twenty feet from the pierhead to enjoy nature's show, four people appeared out of nowhere. Yes, they obviously walked along the pier just as I had done thirty minutes earlier, only I had not noticed until now. The waves regained my full attention, until one of the four walked dangerously close to the pier's edge. One moment I was drinking in the lake's playfulness, and the next I had begun to plan where I would throw my wallet and iPhone before diving into the lake to save this person who was sure to be swept away. *She is my age, maybe a bit older. She should know better. Can she swim?*

And in the moment that followed, the unexpected happened. Less than two feet from the cement's edge, she opened a small plastic bag and poured the powdery contents into the water. Well, some made it into the water; the rest landed on the pier. She quickly retreated back to avoid the incoming wave. I felt relieved, and I also realized what was taking place.

"Who are you throwing in?" I asked.

Five years earlier my son and I had emptied a bag of similar cremation ashes at a location on Purdue's campus that I refuse to confess in writing. It was one of the to-do-when-I'm-gone items on my father-in-law's yellow legal pad. (Clue: He still attends every home football game.)

Back on the pier, the four folks chuckled at my question and shared that they came from different cities across the country to fulfill their parents' request to have their ashes released into Lake Michigan.

Before the others took their turns, they explained that the original request had come from Mom, who died eight years earlier. One daughter explained that her mother's wishes were clear. "She told us 'With the wind at your back, throw me into the water at the mouth of Grand Haven's pier.'"

They delayed, however, when Dad told the kids, "Don't you dare throw Mom in there until you can throw me in too. She can't swim."

I suggested that they make a quarter turn to the right and face the other side of the channel instead of straight out into the lake. Another daughter stepped forward for her turn and took my advice. I asked, "Which way is the wind now blowing?"

"It's in my back. Wonder why Mom wanted it this way?" she said.

"You had a wise mom," I said. "If you faced any other way, the ashes would blow on you instead of into the water." We all laughed.

"Why this pier?" I asked.

"Dad asked Mom to marry him on this spot many, many years ago."

As the breeze continued to blow, I shivered with appreciation for the chance to witness a truly holy moment for this family. In turn, each of the others took a deep inhale that seemed to fill their hearts and minds with tender memories of two people they loved and deeply missed, then stepped forward and dumped their small bags.

After the last sibling had done so, the best part happened. Two unusually large waves hit the end of the pier, one after the other, both sounding like the boom from a bass drum. Water thoroughly washed all the ashes off the concrete, and spray went at least twenty feet in the air. For that same moment, the sun stood at the perfect angle to cause two rainbows to form. Although each lasted only a second or so, their brilliance stayed long enough to be appreciated—and remembered—for breathtaking beauty and crispness. Colors so big, so bright, yet so close. High definition beyond explanation. Not once, but twice.

I broke the reverent silence. "All is well out there," I declared, still looking across the waves.

"One rainbow for Mom, and one for Dad," a daughter quietly added. "How fitting; they so loved each other."

They turned and began the walk back to their cars, mission accomplished. I remained; the truly sacred moment this family allowed me to join just had to continue a minute or so longer. Many times my hard heart, stubbornness, and numerous other character deficiencies qualify me to be swept off that pier. Pushed off, actually. Standing there, scanning the wave-frothed water for the answer to some unaskable question deep within me, a priority for life became clear: to be remembered as a person who steadfastly showed up for and "so loved" my wife.

After all, that's what I promised Becky and Dave. And it seems like that's exactly what Lou keeps saying, too.

Love never fails.

CHAPTER 8

CHOICES, CHOICES

Sometimes the hardest person to show up for is yourself.

The world changes, one life at a time, through love and hope. People share love because God first loved us, but where does hope have its start?

Answer: In the dark.

Specifically, the moments in life when darkness and defeat settle in and seem to win the day, or maybe just bully us for a while. Eventually we reach the point where we sigh and want to give up—but then a light pokes through, illuminating other options. Or maybe just one. That light is hope.

Hope is the belief that circumstances will change, that tomorrow will be better—it's our reason to try again. To keep going is a choice that helps us fully engage life rather than hide from it.

Hope experienced becomes hope to share, but first comes a choice.

On the final point of my sixteen-year-old daughter Erin's regional tennis tournament, the ball bounced low off her racquet and landed in the net. Her eyes pinched closed in an attempt to hide from the moment. "Please, no," she whispered to herself, wishing the situation away.

After a slow walk past the errant ball to meet her opponent at the net for an obligatory handshake and forced smile, every breath required extra effort while she gathered her gear and shoved it into her equipment bag. Self-disappointment wrapped its mean arms around her and squeezed low and tight.

It showed. Why wouldn't it? A season of loss after loss had ended. But the end brings no solace when a person keeps going, hoping to turn a corner—and instead runs out of road. Months of hard work on the court when friends were at the beach, early morning and late night workouts, weeks of dreams and prayers—all seemed wasted. Lost in a fog of frustration, feeling that life was moving like a river flowing against her, Erin trudged off the court into the crowd of players and parents.

A familiar voice cut through the noise. It was her dad.

"Let's take a walk."

The light crunch of steps on grass and gravel were the only sounds for several minutes, except for a few sniffs. Even on a face soaked with perspiration, tear trails are easy to spot. In such a moment, the best words are no words.

The silence continued until she took a deep breath to muster a labored whisper, "This isn't worth it anymore. All I want to do is quit."

It was hard to fall short once again. It was hard to lose on a day she had waited for and prepared for her entire season. It was hard to drop another match she could have won. It was easy to feel completely defeated in this moment and believe that hard work is for fools. Darkness might have claimed another victory had Erin walked alone.

"It only ends now if *you* decide it does," Dad said. "Your choice."

Hope is the realization that giving up is just one option— and that others exist. One of the greatest challenges everyone faces is not failure; it's the desire to quit. Whether in a sport, school, workplace, or a relationship, walking away tempts us all.

Tough moments can also have equal chances to become defining moments. Erin chose to not quit. To not accept this day as the end of the road. To keep going. She just needed to hear another option.

When facing challenges, a person learns whether she can count on herself to show up and show resilience. Such resiliency, in fact, offers some of life's best opportunities.

Maju has a heart to help people, so she earned an associate's degree and started a nursing career. Soon, she longed for the chance to work in her local hospital's emergency room, and for several years applied every time there was an opening. Unfortunately, nurses with more experience or education consistently received the job offers. Maju knew that without work opportunities she couldn't change her experience level so, instead, she focused on adding to her education.

A nearby university offered an ideal program for career nurses in pursuit of their bachelor's degree. Many other caregivers take this route for the same reasons as Maju. So many, in fact, that the school accepts only a portion of the applications received.

As a member of this college's community board of advisors, I talk with groups of students to better understand their experiences. During one such gathering I met Maju. My standard list of questions includes asking students to share why they selected this program. Most responses focus on the school's reputation. Maju concurred, although she added a matter-of-fact statement that grabbed my attention.

"That's why I applied eight times."

"Wait," I said. "You applied to this place eight times?"

"Sure did."

"Why?"

"I just didn't want to give up when all it might take was trying one more time."

I really can't recall any other comments made that afternoon. Instead, I let myself enjoy the rush of feeling swept away from hearing something profound, offered by someone with such abundant hope that she shares it without trying. Did she even know the significance of what she said?

Think of the work required to apply for college admission, especially those feelings of accomplishment and relief upon completing the forms, finishing the essays, and submitting all the needed paperwork. Then the dark and silent, nearly cruel, waiting period—eventually broken by a rejection notice. A form letter. It's impersonal. It could make all the time and effort seem wasted. And it might seem like the end of the road.

But not for this candidate.

Eight applications. Seven "thanks, but no" responses. Most of us would yield to defeat and begrudgingly move on after just a couple of turn-downs, feeling wounded—and definitely resentful toward the school, the admissions office, and nurses everywhere, right? Oh, I know how my mind would try to spin the situation: *I didn't want to go there anyhow*. Bitterness seems like a much-needed drink when parched by rejection. Unfortunately, it's a gulp of seawater that messes you up even worse.

Common sense says that only a fool stands at the door knocking after hearing, "Go away!" But to believe that such a voice speaks the final answer rids a life of many opportunities, especially those unlocked by commitment. Resiliency, on the other hand, whispers, "But what if?" and then reminds a person that circumstances will change… that tomorrow will be better… that eventually the door will open. So keep knocking.

Maju looked embarrassed to share her story in front of peers. To spare her further discomfort, I waited until after the meeting to tell her, "In life, lucky people do well. Bright and talented people do great. The rare individual willing to keep trying, one more time, over and over, is the kind of person who changes the world. You, clearly, are one of the rare ones."

Plenty of people will benefit when a nurse named Maju, who knows how to keep hope alive, shows up for them.

Inside every person, the place that gives birth to hope also houses a deep desire to live. I saw that choice made up close and personal. Too close, actually.

The nightstand clock glowed unwelcome numbers: 2:15. At that hour of the morning, sleep is all that matters. Yet I couldn't. Something woke me. While waiting for my senses to catch up with my consciousness, the reason became clear—my wife Becky.

After spending twenty-five years with someone, rhythm changes draw attention. An expression, a sigh, a misstep—all command fresh notice. In this case, her breathing was different. So was her body temperature. Everything about her, in fact, seemed off normal. Way off. A gentle you're-having-a-bad-dream-so-wake-up nudge changed nothing. In fact, she seemed to labor more with every inhale and exhale.

"Becky? Becky?" I said while pushing her shoulder.

No response from her. I, on the other hand, responded quite well to the adrenaline now surging through my body. The sheet and blanket landed on the floor at the same time as my feet. The cold hardwood provided enough traction to enable a long-step over the linen pile and stretch for the light switch.

As the lamps screamed light into the room, my eyes focused on my unusually pale wife. It was almost as if she wore cheap grey make-up. The cringed expression that accompanied her every breath confirmed that this was no bad dream.

Actually, this felt like a nightmare.

My hand reached for her neck to check for a pulse. Any pulse. Please, a pulse. What a relief to feel small surges in her veins. Or were they arteries? I didn't care; I'm no nurse but I know it was a pulse. Quite a rapid one, in fact.

Bad dreams might make a heart race, but they typically don't turn a person's skin grey and replace breathing with wheezing. Why wouldn't she wake up? Unsure what to do, I shook her and yelled her name. Four shakes later, she opened her eyes.

While my senses were on uber-alert, hers remained nearly out of order. But she now breathed better. My mind estimated that a trip to the emergency room would take less than five minutes, so that was the plan. Eight steps down the hallway, I opened my daughter's bedroom door and turned on her light switch.

"Something's wrong with Mom," I said, speaking slowly and trying to sound composed. "Get dressed and help me with her; we're leaving for the hospital in thirty seconds."

Some messages cut through the air like a chainsaw no matter how calm the delivery.

Fortunately, early morning adrenaline must run through the family DNA because Erin arrived in our bedroom an instant after my return. A few moments later, we clicked the seatbelt around Becky.

I have zero recollection of the drive. Based on the arrival time printed on the emergency room report, it went fast.

Several questions, examinations, tests, and monitors later, the physician described how Becky's heart had gone out of rhythm and needed help returning to normal. A quick procedure called a cardio-version would take care of it. Neither Becky nor I fully understood what would take place next, but I should've expected something significant when the nurse told my daughter to leave the room. "Spouse can stay if you want," she said to me.

Of course I wanted to stay. This is my wife who has stood beside me through tough times. After watching her give birth to our son and daughter, what could be more challenging to witness?

In hindsight, I probably should've left the room.

As the hospital's trauma team disconnected her oxygen and monitors, then attached new lines coming from a special cart, a "cardio-version" began to look like a big deal.

Becky signed a liability release form, and within two blinks of an eye the physician injected a frothy white drug into her intravenous line. One last blink and she went unconscious—an all-too-familiar sight this morning. The doctor shouted her name and gave her a shake. No response.

"She's out. Let's go with fifty," he said.

"Okay, fifty," the head nurse replied.

Fifty what? The machine on the trauma cart started to sound like a jet powering up engines at takeoff.

Just a few seconds later, the nurse began to count numbers with the same strong, yet composed voice I used when waking my daughter.

"48…49…50. Everyone clear!"

Four people standing at Becky's bedside took a fully synchronized step backwards. Before I could even wonder why, the nurse pushed a large button on the machine.

The sound a defibrillator makes when delivering an electrical charge mimics that of a car falling off a jack. Powerful. Piercing. Unexpected. The sight of what happens as a result overshadows the disturbing sound. My wife's body lurched up and down, completely rising off the bed. Her eyes bulged open in a lifeless stare.

Then the most troubling of all sounds filled the room. Her heart rate monitor, beeping as background noise since we arrived, now let out a monotone wail.

In layman's terms, a cardio-version stops a patient's heart so it can regroup and then start again, ideally in a normal rhythm. As the only layman in the room, I'm convinced my heart also stopped as I waited for a beep. Any beep. Please beep.

Becky's heart faced a decision. Remain stopped. Or start again. Call it quits. Or choose to live.

She made a wonderful choice. Beep. Beep. Beep. She chose life.

Later that morning, the physician said their team had performed the same procedure a few hours earlier on another patient. He considers them quite routine.

Life is so momentary and filled with choices. Many qualify as routine. Others pack more voltage. The best choices though, unleash the inner hope that drives us—and also encourage us to interrupt our own lives in order to show up for someone else.

The internal-external relationship is simple: show up for yourself so you can show up for others. Prove to yourself that you have what it takes to keep going, that you're able to commit to something important, and that you're full of life. Then share all of that life with others. You can only give away what you already have.

Overflow with hope.

CHAPTER 9

I WANNA DANCE

Sometimes, showing up for others requires the willingness to go where you've never gone and do what you've never done.

"I'll tell you what's wrong these days," said Lou. "People are too busy to stop and help other folks."

People who know me well recognize my tendency toward stubbornness, although I don't see it and never will. Okay, maybe a little. Anyhow, a couple decades ago I heard a speaker espouse the value of solitude as a way to relax and gain perspective, an outlook that only comes to people willing to slow down and escapes life's many noises. To abscond from all that distracts. Linger on a thought or two. Then listen for—and to—God's gentle whisper. That last one's hard, for sure. Especially for people considered stubborn, because they already have a good idea about what they want to hear. Or so I am told.

I decided to give solitude a serious try. A nearby forest preserve served as a convenient location for a monthly dip into seclusion. I soon realized that speaker knew what she was talking about; the relaxation I experienced in a couple hours alone definitely outweighed the teeth gnashing I went through to block off time on my schedule.

Six months into this new routine, on a stroll along my now-familiar walking path, I took a fresh approach to my time alone. For a solid hour, I mentally scrolled through a set of personal attributes found in the Bible—love, joy, peace, patience, kindness, goodness, faithfulness, gentleness, and self-control. The list looped over and over, powered by a single question: How true is each of these in my life? Wandering along the wooded path lost in self-examination, I wondered: *Why not say the list out loud? After all, no one is around.*

So I walked and spoke each attribute aloud, one at a time. The squirrels likely thought I sounded nuts. At the very point I said "kindness," the lone stop sign along the path appeared out of nowhere and ran into me. Or am I too stubborn to admit I walked into it? Either way, the collision caused me to abandon the list and focus on that one word.

Kindness. Kindness. Am I kind? I want to think so. But kindness is not what one thinks; it's a result of what one does. So the question became, *Do I show kindness to others?* The honest answer hurt to admit: *No. Oh, how I wish I had stopped on "joy".* Solitude, I learned, creates space for truth to show up.

After another hour of focus on that lone word, and the unpleasant feeling from conviction of a character deficiency, I left the woods on a quest to show kindness—a journey I felt ill-equipped to navigate. Okay, I felt lost. Until, that is, I attended our church's midweek service the next evening and read a small blurb in the bulletin that began with the words "Share kindness."

Oh that's good, God. That is really good. Funny, actually. Okay, you have my attention.

A ministry needed volunteers willing to personally partner with children who have special needs. The next day I called Kaleen, the ministry director, to learn more. A few days later, we met. She explained how the program works and asked if I would prayerfully consider helping a young boy on her waiting list. At some point, too subtle to notice, her request morphed into my commitment to active duty, because by the time our meeting ended, I had agreed to show up the next Sunday morning to meet Jimmy and his parents.

My life was about to change.

While standing—okay, pacing—by the door to the second- and third-graders' room, self-doubt felt like a tight jacket that shrank a full size every minute that passed. *I really don't know what to do. What if he doesn't like me? I'm not qualified, trained, or competent in any way to care for a child with physical challenges. I'm not even breathing well right now. What if I do something wrong? I feel dizzy.*

A couple of deep breaths followed by more anxious pacing and thoughts racing. *How does this have anything to do with kindness? Don't kindness and happiness travel together? I can't believe Kaleen talked me into this!*

Five minutes after the children's program began, a new thought offered temporary relief: *Maybe they're not coming! Showing up counts toward kindness points, right?*

A moment later, the whining came to a stop when Jimmy and his parents arrived. We exchanged pleasant greetings as all of us scanned the hallway for Kaleen. Jimmy's mom broke the awkward silence and described in a matter-of-fact tone how cerebral palsy affected her son's legs and right arm. He had spent his whole life in a wheelchair, so it served as a very safe and comfortable place for him. "Actually, it's part of him," she said.

I nodded as if I understood, yet really didn't. Or couldn't. In a world where even slight physical dissimilarities can place a child on the outside of the social circles, it was impossible to imagine the isolation felt by someone with more extreme differences, like a wheelchair. Loneliness can grip anyone, of course, but extends an especially warm welcome to persons who stand (or sit) furthest from the "like everyone else" standard. I was beginning to understand that kindness sometimes arrives through a slight tear of the heart.

After surprisingly few care instructions, Jimmy's mom and dad said goodbye and headed to the church service. There I stood and he sat. A bewildered young boy and an equally unsure adult looked at one another, both silently wondering, *What now?* Obviously, the answer was nowhere to be found in the hallway, so I pulled the room door open as far as the hinge allowed, pushed Jimmy's chair, and our adventure together began.

Inside the very large and somewhat chaotic room filled with children involved in all sorts of crafts and games, we spent a few minutes getting to know one another. Jimmy described the limits of his legs and arm, highlighting the strength of the arm the cerebral palsy had missed. He even suggested an arm-wrestling challenge—and smiled with delight following three quick victories. I could've taken him but didn't want to hurt him; a wheelchair makes its occupant seem quite fragile.

The lights dimmed a couple times, then a voice over the sound system told everyone to find their small group designated by primary colors. We wheeled over to a cluster of second graders sitting on the floor, the Yellow Team. The moment we arrived, the room lights went dark and a stage lit up.

Music plays a key role in children's ministry, and songs typically include motions that kids find fun because they involve legs, arms, hands, and sometimes their whole bodies. The singers on stage, accompanied by a small band already playing, asked everyone to stand for the first song. *Well this sure feels awkward.*

As the band continued playing intro chords, the lead singer refreshed everyone's memory about key motions for the first song. The arm motions? Not for Jimmy. The hopping side to side? Nope. So we continued to sit and watch. *Please make this stop soon.*

This little guy struggles through scores of battles every day; to get in and out of a car, enter a building without an automatic door, navigate tight restaurant tables, use the bathroom, the list runs long. And now, in church, another clear reminder about the limits of wheelchair-bound living.

To help Jimmy not feel alone, I remained seated on the floor next to him. He might look different. He might feel different. But he was not going to experience loneliness.

Cerebral palsy has no cure, but just one person can remedy the sting from feeling lonely.

Once the full song began, the band certainly played a catchy beat. The entire roomful of kids knew when to hop on beat three times to the left, then three to the right. The choreography was compelling, no doubt, and made everyone want to join in. Except, of course, kids in wheelchairs. For them, there was no way to participate. Or was there? Jimmy had an idea.

"I wanna dance," he told me as the high-energy tune continued.

"You want to what?" I shouted so he could hear me over the music.

He reached down with his strong arm, unlocked his chair's wheels, and unfastened his seat belt. He shouted back, "Pick me up!"

Yes, this kid's a warrior. Me? Not so much. The anxious thoughts returned and squeezed me tight. *What if I hurt him? Will other people be alarmed? Or think I'm weird? This won't work. I can't dance. His parents didn't say we could do this. Neither did Kaleen. Where is she, anyhow? Oh, please let the music stop.*

"C'mon. Pick me up, I wanna dance!"

Was this a moment God had in mind all along? Probably so, but likely a moment for Jimmy's sake more than mine.

The time had come for me to do what someone else needed done. Kindness takes place best when you just give in and let it happen.

The best place to pick him up was to reach under his arms from behind and lift. I didn't figure this out on my own; he communicated with clarity by flapping both arms. So up he went as if a forklift had grabbed him. Once he cleared his chair, we began to move to the beat with everyone else. Three hops to the right, pause, three hops to the left.

The energy from his joy arced between us. Hop, hop, hop. Throughout the song, I held Jimmy in front of me and served as his legs. Hop, hop, hop. Because I have the rhythm of a flat tire, we fought hard to keep up with the music. We knocked into other kids. We looked silly. Hop, hop, hop.

Three songs later, the music ended and Jimmy landed back in his chair exhilarated. I sat down on the floor, soaked with perspiration and completely winded. "That was awesome!" he said.

And awkward. And strenuous. And really hard on my back. Life is like a song; to some it's an opportunity to dance, to participate, and to feel great joy. For others it's a challenge, because for whatever the reason, they can only watch others move and hop and have fun. But Jimmy's triumphant smile gave me new perspective and impressed upon my heart a deep desire—a direction to follow the rest of my life. A purpose. And it all started with his words: "I wanna dance. Pick me up."

That's it: *I want to help people dance*. To pick them up. Stand beside them. Sit if needed. Show up with a smile and kind words. Even if it lasts only a brief moment, what a thrill it is to stop along life's path, to step out of your story and into someone else's, and help someone dance. To play a part, big or small, as they rise up and out of limitations life has forced upon them—or maybe from dealing with loneliness—and feel joy. Just the way life should work. Especially when it's not my idea. Or convenient. Or easy. Or about me.

Serve one another humbly in love.

CHAPTER 10

THE PRESIDENT, A PASTOR, AND A PHYSICIAN

S howing up for people requires noticing them.

"You must keep your immune system strong to help you win this fight, so eliminate stress."

Of all the information shared during my first oncology visit, those words offered me hope. Everything else sounded truly frightening. My oncologist's directive on stress gave me something to do with high purpose. He had handed me a secret weapon to fight back against the cancer. Let the battle begin.

Four months following surgery for advanced melanoma and four weeks after surviving experimental drug therapy, an unexpected fever arrived. A few other unwelcome symptoms also showed up. Apparently my immune system had decided to sit out part of the fight, which led to my doctor's conclusion, "This appears likely to be lymphoma. We'll need to run tests to confirm."

Unfortunately, the lymphoma news arrived a few days ahead of another major tension source. Life seemed to have confiscated my secret weapon.

At the time, I worked as the communications director for my suburban Chicago church, a position with responsibilities for a team of writers and graphic designers, as well as spokesperson duties to the media and public. When issues arose, the church expected my full involvement and best efforts. So when a call came to attend an urgent meeting to discuss an upcoming major event, it felt like business as usual—even though the rest of life felt rather unusual. Cancer does that to a person.

About a dozen people sat in the conference room waiting for Bill, our senior pastor, to join us via conference call. Still no big deal. *I have lymphoma, so I hope whatever this is doesn't need much of me.* My internal self-dialogue distracted me so much I failed to hear the phone ring. But the couple minutes that followed commanded my entire attention, because the most long-lasting leadership moment I've ever experienced took place.

Through the speakerphone, Bill asked for the names of everyone gathered to meet. After the roll call, he said, "Dave, my assistant Jean tells me you have some new health concerns. How are you doing?"

Caught a bit off guard, I replied, "I'm okay today. Looks like my battle wants to continue, though."

"Is there anything I can do; any way I can help?"

"No, Bill. I have a great doctor on this, so I'm good. Thanks, though."

"Well count on my prayers and let me know if you need anything. And I mean anything. Alright everyone, we have some other business to attend to."

When a leader deliberately makes someone else a priority—even for just a moment—it places a permanent handprint on that person's heart. Why? Because to notice and acknowledge communicates a desire to care. That brief exchange, which lasted less than ninety seconds, has shaped more of my own leadership and relationship decisions than any other moment in my adult life.

If that seems like an over-dramatized statement, it may make more sense in light of the "other business" we attended to during the meeting: The President of the United States had agreed to speak at an upcoming church event just two weeks away. And for reasons I still don't know, Bill named me the church's point person to coordinate all details between the church and the White House, Secret Service, and media. Yes, during the two weeks coinciding with my fresh and urgent journey through the healthcare system.

You must keep your immune system strong to help you win this fight, so eliminate stress. What a joke.

The next thirteen days felt surreal. Phone calls with the White House Press Secretary's office. Multiple facility tours with the local Secret Service team. Doctor appointments and tests. Why did the President and lymphoma have to arrive simultaneously? In fairness to Bill, I did receive the option to take a pass. On coordinating the President's visit, not the lymphoma. Some adventures, though, are just too good to miss. And this one certainly fell in that category.

Again I mean the President's visit, not the lymphoma.

Preparation for a presidential speaking engagement is both intense and thorough. In addition to protection for the President, the security blanket would wrap around a few people at the host site, specifically the host (Bill) and the public spokesperson (me). One question asked by the Secret Service made me laugh: "Has anyone ever threatened you, harmed you, or you believe could pose any threat?"

Immediately, a few mean kids from grade school came to mind, including my brother. As did a couple of annoying neighbors. If those names were shared, would they be temporarily detained? Or handcuffed? Oh, the temptation.

Instead I grinned and said no. Then, for the next several minutes, I had to explain the grin. Clearly, there was no room for humor in all this for the Secret Service.

The process to confirm lymphoma proved equally tense. Waiting for appointments to start. Waiting for test results. Waiting to discuss next steps. Fortunately, I had plenty to occupy all this time. Once, while my wife and I sat in an exam room, the President's Assistant Press Secretary called my cell phone with a question. A moment later, the doctor entered the room. My wife asked him to please not talk because I was on the phone with the White House. She laughed at the crazy timing. My doctor didn't laugh. Clearly, there's not much room for humor when it comes to cancer, either.

Finally, the day of President Clinton's visit arrived. In our final briefing, I met the Secret Service agent assigned to accompany me throughout the day. We shook hands, he gave me a name badge and special pin that allowed me access throughout the facility, and I asked if he would show me his gun and any other weapons. Not even a grin; just a stare through dark sunglasses.

As the auditorium where the President would speak filled, members of the media arrived and took their places in a specially designated area. Except, that is, for one photographer. He took a seat in the center section, second row. A great angle for a picture, no doubt. But if he was allowed to go wherever he wanted, then the rest of the press would do the same.

When I tapped him on the shoulder and explained that he needed to return to the media section, he dismissed me, saying, "I don't care, I'm staying."

I was no media relations specialist, just a church spokesperson, and I felt embarrassingly ill-prepared. As I tried to find just the right words to repeat my request, the agent assigned to me told me he'd handle the situation. With his steel hand firmly gripping the photographer's shoulder, he said, "Sir, step out into the aisle right now and follow Mr. Staal's instructions or you will be immediately detained."

The agent's words worked well. My grin returned. For a moment I regretted not sharing the names of the mean kids, my brother, and those neighbors. With all of the now-eager-to-cooperate media representatives in place, next stop was the parking lot. Another memorable moment awaited.

In addition to coordination duties, Bill assigned me and my colleague Scott the privilege to officially greet the President. As the presidential caravan neared the church, Scott and I took our positions marked on the sidewalk. Several police cars, SUV's, and limos arrived as we all stood perfectly still. No matter how many times I wiped my hand on my pants leg, the perspiration stayed. Lymphoma, what lymphoma? One of those cars holds the most important leader on the planet, whom I will soon meet—and my hands wouldn't stop oozing sweat.

The doors of the SUV's and all but one limo opened, agents emerged, and in choreographed fashion, took positions that surrounded and fluidly moved toward the President's car. He stepped out, walked straight to me, and grabbed my moist hand. His was enviably dry, almost as if powdered. Before I could say the greeting I had rehearsed for hours, he spoke first: "David, it's great to finally be here and meet you!"

His warmth and casualness sounded almost as if we were already friends! Did someone tell him about all the work I put in for his visit? I must have made quite the impression on the press secretary and his staff.

"Welcome to Willow Creek, Mr. President."

"Thank you David. Now who do we have here?"

I hadn't rehearsed saying Scott's name. In fact, I couldn't remember his name, even though we had worked closely together for a couple years. Fortunately, he remembered his own name and introduced himself.

The President continued to walk toward the building where Bill and others also greeted him. When he was a safe distance away, I said to Scott with a big smile, "I can't believe he knew my name!"

"Dave, you're wearing a name badge."

Even the Secret Service agent grinned behind his glasses.

Too often, greetings come off as mechanical. While it might seem unimportant or inconsequential, extending warmth and focused attention that makes someone feel special creates a moment that will last a long time. Both my pastor and the President had done exactly that—and any of us can do the same. You and I can always put in momentary extra effort to help people feel good. Such gestures give people a brief portal out of everyday life and all its challenges.

Maybe the world would be a friendlier place if everyone wore name badges.

Life and all its challenges tried to catch up with me when, a few minutes later, my cell phone rang. Test results were now available, so an appointment was set for the next day. No time to worry about them, though; there was business to attend to.

Following the President's departure, the media gathered in a meeting room for a debrief. To quickly prepare for my first and only press conference with local and national news outlets, I met with Bill in his office. After we talked through a couple of statements to share with reporters, he asked a question that communicated his keen awareness for the challenges I faced. "Can you think of anything else I can do to help you?"

When a leader willingly reverses roles with someone in his or her charge, a priceless dynamic occurs that earns respect, commitment, and a spot in long-term memory. Experts overcomplicate servant-leadership, yet it's simple to see in action when done with authenticity.

"Do you want to meet the press?"

"Oh no. That's what I pay you to do. I have complete confidence you'll do fine."

"Okay, then there is one thing. I'd like to tell everyone you've gone home so I don't have to argue about why they can't hear directly from you."

"Are you telling me to leave?"

"Bill, I'd rather not lie. So yes, I'm asking you to go home."

With a big smile he said, "We've been honest so far. Let's keep it up. I'll leave right now."

I'll always remember the day I kicked the senior pastor out of our church.

The next morning I appeared live on a 6 a.m. network news broadcast to discuss the President's visit. Although the show's producers preferred to talk with our senior pastor, I was the only option because he remained unavailable—as a favor to me. No, I didn't tell him to stay home. Rather, just come in later than usual. So there I stood, in front of a camera, wearing an earpiece and a microphone while answering questions posed remotely by the news anchors from their studio in downtown Chicago. I felt a bit less bold than the day before because my agent friend was long gone. Now I listened and responded to questions with just one part of my brain, while the other half wondered what news waited for me from the doctor.

After several hours of media interviews, all went quiet. Such is the ADHD nature of the news. Needing a break from the sound of my own voice, I listened to a music CD while driving to my doctor's downtown Chicago office and tried—unsuccessfully again—to eliminate the stress I felt.

Looking around the waiting room at the oncology office served as an unwelcome reminder about how, with all due respect, insignificant the President seems in the world of people battling for their lives. Although I had to admit that the previous two weeks, especially the day before, did serve as an effective distraction from reality.

Linda, the head nurse, greeted me in her typically dry fashion. As we walked to the consultation room, she mechanically asked me how I'd been—even though only a week had passed since seeing one another. "Linda, I met the President yesterday," I said.

Uncharacteristic for her, she grinned and said, "Yeah, right. We'll be in room three."

Soon afterward, my doctor entered the room, flashed his big smile, warmly shook my sweat-soaked hand, and sat down. We had business to attend to.

"I watched the news at breakfast this morning. You and I have very different views about what it means to eliminate stress. Anyhow, I'm glad we could talk in person because I have good news to share. All the tests confirm you don't have lymphoma."

In just twenty-four hours, I heard memorable words from the President of the United States, the pastor of one the largest churches in America, and my physician. Thanks to the third conversation, I've had many years to appreciate— and try to emulate—what I learned from the first two.

Therefore encourage one another and build each other up.

CHAPTER 11

THERE'S SOMETHING IN THE FOOD

Eating provides strength to face life's ups and downs.

Lou loves to talk about his house, probably because he built it. During the 1950s, every day after his factory shift ended and all day on weekends, he constructed the home he would live in for six decades. He created the plans, made every measurement, served as carpenter, mason, electrician, plumber, and even visionary. (In the aftermath of a school demolition, he salvaged several massive wood beams to run the length of his house, supporting the roof.) Few people build like that anymore; their own dwelling made with their own hands.

Lou might occasionally forget my name, but he still thoroughly knows his house's every nuance. Just the mention of a door, wall, or window causes him to lean forward and talk faster, giddy as he recalls details and specifications—

even if the conversation begins with someone else's home.

"A friend had water in his basement from all the recent rain," I told him.

"When I built this house I used the larger size cement blocks in the basement to give it a nine-foot ceiling," Lou replied. "Did I ever tell you that I built this house myself?"

"You've mentioned it before, but tell me how you did it," I said to encourage conversation on a topic that always makes him smile with satisfaction from a job well done.

"When we moved in, I hadn't finished the basement. Not even the staircase. One day as I climbed down the extension ladder to work on it, I fell and broke several bones. Laid there a long time until Ruth figured out what happened and could get help. Finally put that staircase in, though."

Unfortunately for Lou, falling was in his future as well as his past. Over the span of a couple months, tumbles happened with increasing frequency in the bathroom, bedroom, and kitchen; recovery proved difficult. Not a surprise for a ninety-one-year-old man, but the physical strain caused his health to diminish. Soon he lacked the energy and ability to prepare meals—an issue that became the focus during my visits.

If someone says he hasn't had food all day, it's hard to think about anything other than giving him something to eat. A few times this involved a quick trip to a deli for chicken dinners. Other times, my wife prepared extra-large portions for dinner, so I could bring the excess to Lou. Pride made him balk at the help. But hunger would eventually win.

His family wisely suggested he move to an assisted living facility. Lou didn't like the idea. "This is my home and I want to stay here. I'm comfortable here and get around just fine. Did I ever tell you I built this house myself?"

"You must have done a great job for it to still look this good," I said.

"So why would I give all this up for one of those places where you just wait to die?"

The day we met, Lou told me that he spent every day at home, alone, waiting to die. To bring that conversation up now, though, would invite an unnecessary argument. Sometimes a person needs someone to show up and gently offer an option, rather than tell you that what you think, do, or feel doesn't make sense.

Yes, to leave the house he built with his own hands—the place that holds a life's worth of memories and that feels most comfortable—likely seemed close to impossible. No words can erase those realities. But a few other considerations might open the door to possibility.

"It would be nice to have someone prepare all your meals so you don't have to," I offered. "And the place your family found is even closer to my house, so I'll definitely visit you every week. You'll make new friends there, too."

Who knows what role our conversation played in helping him make the decision to leave home. But to everyone's relief, he did. I lived up to my word to make weekly visits, complete with apple pie and coffee. Fortunately, his room is on the first floor and involves no stairs. Unfortunately, the facility has let Lou down on the meals.

"You know this pie you bring messes me up," Lou said between forkfuls during a recent visit.

"How?"

"Well, it reminds me how bad the food is here. They serve us pie and the crust is so hard you couldn't break it if you stepped on it. At every meal all we do is talk around the table about how lousy the food is. Yesterday they served some kinda cheese soup. I can't remember the name of it. Just thinking about it makes me shake more than normal."

"C'mon Lou. Is it really that bad?"

"I tell you what, the guy who runs this place better watch out. People grumble about the food now more than ever. If he doesn't do something soon, there might be a rebellion."

I held my breath for a few moments, knowing that any movement in my chest would allow my suppressed laughter to break free. *What would that look like, Lou? A sit-in strike?*

Maybe it's happening already. The charge of the wheelchair brigade?

Then again, Lou did earn the nickname "Weasel." *I'll keep my thoughts to myself.*

While the snack I bring might fuel an insurrection, it's a chance I willingly take because it strengthens our relational bond. "You know you don't have to bring me anything to eat," Lou said recently. "I've never had this much pie in my entire life."

"Me neither," I said.

"What do you mean?"

"I mean I've never had this much either."

"That's not saying much; I'm almost twice as old as you. You can stop doing it anytime, you know."

"Oh I know. But we both like our time together. We're just two friends talking over pie and coffee."

"Someday I'm going to repay you for all this."

"Lou, you know that our friendship is good enough for me."

My visits become special events when my wife bakes for Lou. When I arrived to an empty room for one of my weekly visits, a nurse told me Lou would return in a few minutes. So I sat outside his door to wait. Soon, an aide pushed Lou in his wheelchair around the corner and down the long hall toward me. Still forty feet away, I could hear their banter.

"That's my good friend. He has a beautiful wife, and I'll bet she made us some pie."

"Well that's exciting."

"C'mon; speed it up a little. I could get there faster by walking."

"You think so, do you?"

"You've never tasted her pie. If you did, you'd race me."

I want to think he's excited to see me, and not just for the apple or banana cream treats. Later that visit, he communicated that this is true—in typical Lou fashion. At the end of our time together, I wheeled him to the dining room for the evening meal. When we arrived at his usual table, he introduced me to the three gentlemen he eats with every day: Glenn, John, and Chester. As I shook their hands, a nurse began to talk with Lou about his medications. While those two chatted, questions came my way.

"So are you his son?" asked John.

"No. Lou and I are just good friends. I come here each week to see him."

"How long have you known each other?" Glenn asked.

"A little over a year."

"What do you do when you come here?" asked John.

"We talk, eat pie, and drink coffee."

"Sure wish I had someone to bring me pie," said Chester.

For as long as I've known Lou, he's had trouble with his hearing. Many times I have to repeat what I've said, even though we sit close. In this moment, though, while he conversed with a nurse, Lou kept one ear tuned to the table talk.

"Oh no you don't, Chester!" Lou said, with the menacing glare of someone who had earned his "Weasel" nickname. "He's my friend, so leave him alone."

Apparently, Lou values our time together as much as he enjoys the pie. Food has a unique special effect; a universal goodwill gesture. When we bring a person something to eat, we share the message, "I care."

Several years ago, another friend, Nancy, proved to my family that she cares a lot. Her jogging route took her past my house, and each day during my month of chemotherapy she stopped to check on me. Many early evenings I sat on the stoop outside our front door to breathe fresh air in hopes my fever would subside. It didn't, but I sure enjoyed it when Nancy would spot me and take a break from exercise to talk. As a former nurse, she asked many questions and gave sound advice.

"You need your energy, so make sure you eat," she said. "What still tastes good?"

The only answer I could think of: chicken.

So the next evening she drove to our house and delivered a very large glass dish. "I hope your family likes this recipe. It's our favorite."

Later that night, my wife counted a dozen large chicken breasts in the pan Nancy brought. "This is an incredible amount of food. Did you tell her that you're struggling to eat?" Becky asked me.

"Not exactly."

Very often, making a big difference for someone else is a progressive process, not simply a single visit or an isolated act. Nancy continued to stop and check on me. My battle with nausea soon became so intense that I wanted my stomach amputated. For a couple days, I couldn't muster the energy to tell Nancy that my appetite for chicken, or anything else, had flown far, far away. She must have been a great nurse, though, because her instincts detected a problem.

"You're not eating," she said.

"I can't." With the only calorie of energy left in me, I hoped she wouldn't ask about the enormous chicken supply my family felt compelled to consume without Papa Bear's help.

She and I chatted about options to try, as well as the anti-nausea medication prescribed to help. It didn't work. Nothing worked. Not even close. Soon, just holding down water became a challenge not worth the effort.

"You're losing weight fast," she said one evening near the end of chemo week three. My conversation ability had long departed, which further encouraged the nurse in her to fully engage.

"What meds do you take?"

I was too weak to remember my own name, much less what pills I took. My wife, though, shared the prescription, and added that I could not keep medicine in my stomach long enough for any benefit. Actually, I could barely swallow. Nancy's next comment would typically cause me to gulp, my eyebrows to raise, and embarrassment to flush my face ketchup red—but only when healthy. That day I felt too sick to react to her words, "Tell them you want an enema."

Nope, didn't expect that. Could a greater contrast exist between that suggestion and the spectacular volume of food she had brought just days before?

Only on the surface. With a closer look, the chicken she brought and the treatment she suggested came from the same place—her genuine compassion for my well-being. And it worked. Within a day, my stomach stopped rejecting everything I swallowed. That helped my strength return which, in turn, enabled me to complete the last five treatments.

The evening after all treatments had ended, Nancy commented that I looked a little better.

"I ate a little chicken," I told her.

She gave me a hug. I whispered, "Thank you for the medication idea," and immediately blushed. I just couldn't say the "e" word.

Nancy put one hand to my cheek and gently ran her fingers down to my chin. She looked deep into my tired eyes and smiled with satisfaction from a job well done. With her final house call now complete, she turned toward the street to continue her jog. As she took her first stride she said, "You're gonna make it."

Fifteen years later, I count Nancy's consistent visits and genuine care as a steady hand I sorely needed to complete my stagger through chemo. Bring food for someone and a door swings open to show up in many ways—and to make a difference long after the last bite.

Recently, I called Lou prior to a visit, and he told me not to come. "The place is locked down," he said. "No visitors allowed. A nasty bug is going around here and almost everyone is sick. I think there was something in the food, but they won't admit it. So stay away until it's safe."

Three days later, my phone rang. "They've opened up again," Lou announced.

"I'll come by tomorrow afternoon," I said.

"Oh, you don't have to make a special trip," Lou said.

"Lou, you know I enjoy our times together."

"Well me too. And don't feel that you have to bring that pie and coffee we like."

"See you tomorrow, Lou."

"I look forward to it, David. I always do."

In our relationship, food plays a big role. But the real reason we get together is to share a slice of life that leaves us smiling with satisfaction. We realize that for now, in this moment, we're gonna make it.

Eat so you have strength for the journey.

CHAPTER 12

WHEN YOU DON'T HAVE TO, DON'T WANT TO

The effort that matters most often takes place beyond what's comfortable or expected.

Even though he had moved from his home into an assisted living facility, Lou continued to shout his typical response to my knock on his door: "Come!"

"Hey Lou, you're looking good today," I said.

"People say that because they feel like they have to, and I hate it when they do," he replied.

"Why do you say that?"

"Because it means I'm not getting any closer to leaving here and going to see my Maker. I don't want to hear I look good—that's going in the wrong direction."

"Okay then, let's start over. Lou, you look like hell."

"Thanks, that's better."

Lou references death with a casualness that seems almost callous. Maybe this attitude came from all the times he watched life end for fellow soldiers. Or from the reality that only very few of his peers still live. Of course, assisted care facilities aren't typically known for their life-giving atmospheres. In the words of 94-year-old George who eats meals with Lou, "This place is just a full service waiting room for the morgue."

My own mortality bothers me little, but the idea of other people dying gives me the creeps. That explains the long inhale/exhale every time I approach the front entrance of the facility where Lou now lives. Or the fear I feel when he doesn't answer the phone when I call. And then call back three times. Maybe a reason for the relationship he and I share is to help me work through this deep discomfort. Showing up for someone affects each party in a unique way. I still have a long way to grow.

I know exactly where this journey began—on a basketball court. As a starter for my high school varsity team, life was good. In Indiana, kids dream of running onto the brightly lit court in a crowded gymnasium on a Friday night, either to hometown cheers or visiting team jeers. That sound, along with the two-part smell of hardwood polish and fresh popcorn, are as easy for me to remember as my own name. Monday through Thursday evening practices, though, proved much less glamorous and are impossible to recall. Except for one.

Teammates Chris, Trent, and I carpooled to practice every day. That car time combined with court time helped the three of us become good friends, even though I was a junior and they were both seniors.

Part way through a Tuesday evening practice, Chris began to shout for our coach's attention. Trent, who had been resting between rotations in a scrimmage, had dropped to the ground. Everyone ran to see what happened. Then, in the shock-induced quiet, we could hear Trent's heavy-labored breaths—shallow and infrequent. My friend, whose smile could light up a dark car on the way home from even the hardest practices, had a face contorted by pain—even though he was clearly unconscious. No movement. No response. Time stood still long enough to burn that moment into my mind. Then it accelerated. Coach made the team leave the gym. We gathered around a water fountain. The police, paramedics, and firefighters arrived. One of our teammates ran up the stairs to the upper decks and we followed. We looked down at the court and no one moved. The two-part sounds of a paramedic repeatedly yelling, "C'mon!" and the defibrillator jolts to my friend will never leave me.

Chris drove crazy fast on the way home that night, and told me he was going to the hospital with his parents. "You going?" he asked.

I wish I had said yes. I wish I had gone to the hospital that night. I wish I had done something; he would've been there for me. But I didn't. Trent didn't make it, either. My friend's heart failed and his life ended that night. In my heart, I failed to show up for him, and I've lived with that disappointment ever since.

The choice to not do something can sometimes haunt us more than things we've actually done. Funny thing about life, sometimes we get a second chance. Mine came three decades later.

Forty-year-old Mike lived with his parents in the house next to ours. He suffered from a disease that progressively destroyed his muscles. His mom and dad provided full-time care for him once he could no longer walk.

He often came outside in his electric wheelchair on summer evenings. During those months, my son Scott and I put on baseball gloves and went on the street to play catch. Mike joined us and provided detailed descriptions of Chicago Cubs games played earlier that day.

I received a phone call on a Sunday afternoon from another neighbor. Mike's parents had taken him to the hospital because his diaphragm muscles no longer worked, meaning he couldn't breathe with his own strength. One week later his parents shared that Mike and the family understood his disease would only get worse, so he wanted all the equipment turned off on Thursday.

We were too busy to go to the hospital Sunday. I made myself too busy on Monday. On Tuesday, I drove past the hospital after a meeting. I was not too busy. Yet I kept driving. *Am I going to show up this time? I really, really don't want to.*

But this time, two better thoughts gripped my heart and wouldn't let go: *It's the right thing to do,* and, *Do it this time.* Similar to the night Trent died, time seemed to accelerate. I remember the drive to the hospital. A long inhale/exhale before I stepped through the door into his room. The sound of a respirator as it forced air through Mike's breathing tube. His smile when he opened his eyes and saw me.

"Don't get up," I said, provoking an even larger grin.

A nurse entered the room to check Mike's monitors and in a friendly tone asked, "Who are you?"

"I'm his dance instructor; he missed his last lesson so I'm here for a private."

She laughed. Mike would've if he could've.

My friend and I spent a few minutes together, alone. Unable to talk, he communicated via a small white board.

He shared thoughts about the journey ahead. We prayed together; I said the words, he squeezed my hands.

"I'm going to leave now," I said. "But I'm not going to say goodbye. Instead, I'm saying 'see ya later.' Do me and Scott a favor—find a street, a ball, and three mitts in heaven. When we join you, we'll all play catch and talk about the Cubs.

"See ya later, Mike."

I left his room and walked a couple steps across the hall and into the elevator; his door remained open. As I pushed the Lobby button, I looked out the elevator into his room and made eye contact with Mike. He mouthed the word "Thanks." The door closed.

Without fail, we will feel thankful every time we show up for someone—especially when we fight through the feeling that we don't want to. Equal satisfaction comes when we don't have to show up for someone but do it anyway. Extra effort can cause great victories. Or at least unexpected wins.

My son Scott entered his senior year of high school football with low expectations. He missed the entire junior season with a broken elbow—a critical injury for a quarterback. The head coach remained uncommitted as to who would earn the starting role, and the anxiety took its toll on Scott's confidence. Then someone showed up for him.

As my son walked to his car after practice, an assistant coach named Dave spotted Scott and asked him to wait a moment. Dave spotted an opportunity to go above and beyond just the X's and O's.

"Several years ago," Dave said, "I coached a quarterback who didn't play his junior year. It wasn't until the next season, when he was a senior, that his chance arrived. Want to know what happened?"

"Sure," Scott said, unsure of where the conversation was headed.

"He had an all-state year and set several single-season records at the school. Want to know why I'm telling you about him?"

"Why?"

"Because you remind me exactly of him. Scott, if you decide you want to, you have what it takes to have a tremendous season. I have no doubt you're every bit as good as he was."

After his own record-shattering year as quarterback, and after receiving all-state honors, Scott credited Coach Dave's words with giving him the fresh, unexpected confidence he needed. At the end of season awards banquet, I thanked Dave for the big difference he made in my son.

"I'm not sure what prompted me to have that talk with him," Dave said, "but I'm sure thankful I did. It wasn't a lot, but look what happened!"

The extra effort to show up for someone with much-needed words, the kind that stick like a fertilizer spike and cause a person's heart to grow, requires little energy. In fact, all you need is two-part willingness: to notice possibility in others and to step out of your preciously held time and into someone else's.

The first place to look? Those closest to you. Late one afternoon, a very young mom showed up in our office with her kindergarten-aged daughter. At first I thought the two were sisters. The mom asked, "When does your next session start?"

I explained that our organization, Kids Hope USA, sets up school-church programs, and that mentors meet with students at school during the school day, meaning we don't actually mentor children in our office. Eager to understand, she shared with me the reason she asked. "My daughter has English as a second language, just like me. She could not go to preschool and I know she needs help now in kindergarten. She is at Roosevelt School. Someone told me that Kids Hope is what she needs."

"All you have to do," I said, "is ask her teacher or the principal for a Kids Hope mentor for your daughter. They've run a program there for years, so they'll know what to do."

"That's all?" she asked.

"Yep, that's it. You should ask soon so that maybe she can have a mentor this school year."

As mother and daughter walked out of our office door and entered the elevator across the hall, she turned with a smile and said, "Thanks!" And the elevator door closed.

Mom might have been in her early twenties, maybe even younger. Do the math for her to have a kindergartner. Yes, this mom looked way too young to have a child in school. I'm sure that people unkindly judge her everywhere they go. But as I looked at her, I saw a mom who's willing to speak up for what her daughter needs, despite her broken English. I saw a mom who wants her daughter to do well in school. I saw a mom bold enough to find out where we're located and show up to ask for help. I saw a mom clearly tired from life, but determined to make life better. I hope someday the daughter appreciates her mom's extra effort.

The deck is stacked against this young lady and her daughter. But mom is willing to ask for new cards. I'm betting on them.

My role at Kids Hope USA requires fairly frequent travel. A recent trip to Colorado routed my trip home through

Dallas. When our delayed flight finally boarded, I sat next to a soldier. *On leave and going home,* I speculated to myself. No, I didn't ask him, because he listened to music in earbuds and I reliably fell asleep within ninety seconds of settling into my seat. No chance for chitchat. We all have our ways.

A little over an hour later, the intercom startled me awake. "We're just waiting for the captain to arrive," said the first officer. "He should be here in the next five minutes."

Wow, we're still in Dallas, I thought. Before I could doze off again, the bad news arrived: "Ladies and gentlemen, the airline has cancelled this flight. Please see the boarding agents in the terminal for new travel arrangements."

Ugh. Not the first time this has happened to me, but it's never welcome. "Well, the captain must have decided to have another drink instead of fly us home," I said in an attempt to lighten the mood for my fellow passengers. I make jokes when I'm travel-weary. We all have our ways to cope.

Instead of a chuckle, the soldier next to me let fly some expletives. *I'll just keep quiet.*

Although I made no attempt to eavesdrop, he spoke so loudly into his phone that I heard him say he probably wouldn't make it home that night. I grabbed my briefcase and started down the aisle toward the door while he still talked. I travel enough to warrant (in my mind) a membership in an airline travel program that allows me to call a service desk where a real person answers the phone. So I called and explained the situation, and in less time than it took to walk off the plane I had a seat confirmed on the next flight. The line at the counter now held all the passengers from our cancelled flight.

"You're lucky you called," she said. "There's only a few more seats on that flight. And the next one is completely full."

"I appreciate your help," I said.

"Is there anything else I can do for you?" she asked.

"No thanks," I said as I walked through the door of a restaurant to start my wait.

When I boarded the next flight, I realized I gave the service rep the wrong answer when she asked if there was anything else I wanted her to do. A quick scan of my fellow passengers, easy to do on a commuter aircraft, showed no sign of the disappointed soldier.

I could have asked the woman on the phone to help the soldier. He serves our country. I'm a beneficiary of his service. I could have helped him make it home. I could have given him a story to tell about a stranger who showed up and helped him. Instead I made jokes. Maybe he would have refused the help. But I didn't even try because I didn't notice anyone other than myself. I still have a long way to grow.

Love your neighbor as yourself.

CHAPTER 13

WHAT IF SOMEONE SHOWS UP?

The world often changes *two* people at a time; one person making a difference in another person's life.

At a Capitol Hill forum focused on the dark and challenging issues facing today's young people, a former gang member shared details of his street life that eventually graduated into youth center incarceration. The event produced contrasting sights in an ironic setting: a 22-year old in jeans and sport shirt describing a life of law breaking to a business-suit clad group of people twice or more his age. All were gathered for a meeting in the Committee on Rules and Administration chamber of the Senate Office Building.

Everyone nodded in agreement with what the young man said, offered forced chuckles at his humor attempts, and wondered why the U.S. Senate could not provide a better air conditioning system.

The hard truth floating through the hot, humid air was that everyone there had heard similar versions of this story many times before. All felt empathy as this young man described detention center conditions. All knew his journey eventually would make a turn for the better—otherwise, he wouldn't have been in that room looking at rows of overheated, overdressed people. Eventually, he shared the resolution to his plight. Following his release from jail a family had taken him in. Nice story. Worth polite applause.

For now, testimony done and solution named. Find stable homes willing to take in young people. Finally, time to find a cup of water on the refreshment table. Surely the Senate would provide ice. But then, just before the session adjourned, an audience member's hand went up. The collective wish: Hope this is an easy question, because that ice will soon melt.

"Would anything have changed if an adult had consistently shown up in your early life, like in elementary school, and encouraged you?"

The young man paused. He thought. His response changed the room's atmosphere like a cool breeze. "I would have made big-time different decisions," he said. "If someone would've been there for me, I wouldn't have needed a gang to feel like someone cared about me. None of this would've happened.

"It's crazy what hope can do," he added.

The truth was out: nothing will change in our young people as a result of more rules and administration. The same applies to middle-aged and older people. Instead, everyone needs a steady source of refreshing encouragement, affirmation, and friendship. In other words, they need hope.

And fortunately, hope is easy to share. At least that's what Karen, a retired but still energetic administrator in Iowa discovered.

She said yes to volunteer as a mentor based on two facts: first, she had time to spend an hour every week at a local elementary school, and second, that school needed more mentors than they had the year before. Apparently, there's no shortage of students who need positive adult relationships. Clearly, this woman is already as informed as a Senator.

So following the application, interview process, and training, Karen received a call from the program director that a little girl at school needed a mentor. She could start right away.

This second-grade student came to school each day wearing a downcast face and refusing to acknowledge people. Even when addressed up close and personally, she offered no response. In fact, she developed deftness at avoiding all eye contact. Instead, she feigned interest in the floor, the wall, a window. After weeks of the teacher's earnest efforts—and similar determination from various specialists—made no progress, the school principal offered a suggestion: let's request a mentor to meet with her.

So just a few days following her call to active duty, the volunteer stood at the door of a second-grade classroom, wondering which girl she was destined to meet. Taking deep, deliberate breaths to minimize the appearance of any nervousness, she remembered to smile. *Are the schools always this warm, or is today unusual?* Who cares; she kept smiling.

Soon the teacher noticed the clearly enthused, slightly nervous lady in the doorway and brought the young girl to meet her mentor.

"You will spend time together every week," the teacher explained.

No response.

"Hi Mia," said Karen. "I'm excited to meet you."

Mia still offered no response.

Before they left the doorway, the teacher handed Karen a sheet of spelling words. "You can try to have her practice writing."

Karen and Mia walked through two hallways, a silent 35-second journey. When they arrived at a vacant office reserved for them, Mia quickly sat in the closest chair at the table as Karen turned on the lights. She walked around the table to sit in the other chair, her back facing the window. She asked Mia several ice-breaker questions learned during her mentor training. No response. The young girl occasionally looked out the window, evading any and all connection attempts. Even on this unusually warm day, the ice refused to thaw.

Question: What's the right thing to do when you show up for someone and nothing happens?

Answer: Stay, wait, and see.

So Karen relaxed, breathing slowly and quietly so Mia would not sense any frustration. Remain in a situation long enough without trying to control it, she reasoned, and room will open for a special moment to arrive.

And indeed it did; triggered by a tender, divinely inspired question.

"Mia, has anyone ever told you that you have beautiful eyes?"

No response—at first. Then slowly, as though dumbfounded by what she had heard, Mia's gaze lifted from the spelling word sheet on the table. Her eyes met Karen's. And a single tear formed.

Before it had a chance to spill down her cheek, Mia quick-stepped from her chair and wrapped her arms around Karen's neck. As she hugged her mentor, between alternating breaths and sobs, she described how everyone at home ruthlessly makes fun of her and that she feels lonely all day every day; she spends all night in her room; nobody at school talks to her; some kids make fun of her, and she has no idea why any of this is the way it is.

And no, no one had ever told her she has beautiful eyes.

But Karen did. Immediately, the two bonded. Over the following weeks, and with plenty of encouragement, Mia opened up to others.

A life can change in a moment. Especially when someone shows up and remains willing to stay around long enough for that moment to happen—maybe within a few minutes… maybe over a few months … maybe even longer. Availability really does trump rules and administration. As does simplicity over complexity.

Let moments happen and then watch what takes place.

What about age? It doesn't matter. After which birthday would the question Karen asked have become unwelcome? The hurting, the lonely, the people wondering whether they matter to anyone inhabit every year of every generation. Many young people, many old, and many somewhere between share a common need: someone to arrive armed only with an ability to care. Even just a little.

In fact, mixing age brackets often creates fresh and unexpected opportunities. Why? Because powerful potential exists when people with no reason to meet actually intersect and stay awhile.

Our world needs more people willing to welcome the possibility that some paths cross due to a grand—or perhaps divine—reason. What a thrill it is to notice those moments when they occur.

For instance, studies show that a child who falls behind after the first grade has a mere one in eight chance of ever catching up with classmates—unless extraordinary measures intervene.

Many children today walk through very challenging lives they neither asked for nor can do much about. Such was the case for Robert, a young student who walked through a rough section of Dallas and a tough childhood every day to attend school. He needed something extraordinary to take place.

By third grade, Robert's reading skills were so far off pace that his principal believed he would likely never graduate. From elementary school. His constant unruliness, leading to frequent appearances in her office, made her prediction easy to accept. The multitude of clever and complex academic intervention programs so often miss the obvious: too many students have holes in their hearts, not holes in their heads. Go ahead and try cramming knowledge into those little minds, but little will stick until they feel loved, cared for—and that they matter to someone.

A reality, by the way, that people never outgrow.

Robert felt none of those things, but then a local church began a partnership with his school, launching a Kids Hope USA mentoring program. His teacher recommended him for the program, and soon Robert began meeting every week for an hour with a volunteer mentor—a very ordinary older man willing to share life's most precious commodity: time.

Cue the extraordinary to begin.

Robert's mentor possesses no skills as a reading development tutor. In fact, if such a competency had appeared in the job description, he wouldn't have bothered to step forward. The simplicity of the role attracted him. So he walks into the school equipped with a big smile and a stubborn belief in the goodness of the little boy he meets every Wednesday afternoon. He encourages Robert to try his best, and affirms his efforts big and small. The two possess little in common; different appearances, different ethnicities, different economics, and vastly different ages— in fact, seven decades separate them. Yet they share an hour together—and that's more than enough for something incredible to happen.

Maybe after a few minutes… maybe a few months… maybe even longer.

Fast forward to fifth grade, attended by a well-mannered boy who no longer wears out his welcome in the principal's office. Instead, Robert now wears a constant smile. His bright-eyed grin acts as a billboard for the condition of his heart.

During a visit to his school, I had the opportunity to meet Robert and his mentor. Robert's principal boasted about him, said she lists him as one of the school's best readers, and shared a guarantee that he'll definitely graduate. From high school. Then she made a very unexpected request.

"Please tell as many people as you can that what happened with Robert is a miracle."

No matter how hard you try, you cannot make a miracle happen for yourself. But you can put yourself in position to help a miracle happen for someone else.

What many people need most in this world is one person, just one, willing to spend time, to offer encouragement, to prove that there *is* someone who cares. Who listens. Smiles. And along the way stubbornly believes in the goodness that exists in every heart—young or old. Someone whose simple presence paints a hope-filled picture of how life could be. Or should be.

When that happens, eventually something extraordinary will happen. And yes, it is a miracle.

Two questions occupied my mind as I walked out of the school that hot Dallas afternoon. How do I live up to the principal's request? And how quickly will the air conditioner cool down my car?

"Wait, please wait for me," I heard.

Robert's mentor caught up with me. As we stood on the sidewalk, perspiring, he reintroduced himself and said he wanted to clarify something. Apparently, he had heard the principal mention a miracle and felt embarrassed at such a claim.

Then, with only the most humble intent, he unknowingly shared a recipe to change the world: "I didn't do anything special. Really. All I did was show up."

Therefore go...

CHAPTER 14

A PIECE OF CHOCOLATE TO LAST A LIFETIME

Oftentimes the least likely becomes the most extraordinary.

Fifth grade treated me well. I enjoyed popularity, earned good grades, and excelled in sports. I occupied one end of the social spectrum. Whether that was the best end remains debatable.

The late elementary school years can prove pretty rough for students on the other end, or even for those right in the middle. Most kids know exactly where they belong and remain there unless something dramatic takes place: typically a growth spurt over summer vacation, contact lenses to replace eyeglasses, or an unexpected kickball home run in gym class. Life continues to work roughly the same for people of all ages.

Furthest from me in the pecking order sat Lori, who had challenges that none of her classmates understood. She even suffered occasional seizures—right there in school. Such moments grab everyone's attention and set a kid apart. She spent every day trapped in an invisible bubble called loneliness that no one entered, with walls too thick for her to escape. Lori seemed fully surrendered to the reality of life lived in her own world; she rarely interacted with others. Not even her teachers.

Too many people live lonely. Yet their bubbles are imaginary and, with deliberate effort applied, none are strong enough to prevent entry. With Lori no one tried, including me. So she remained alone. Unnoticed. But that would soon change.

A week before our class Christmas party, we all lined up single-file to draw names from a box for the annual gift exchange. My turn arrived. I reached in and made a grab. Oh the instant anxiety of reading Lori's name on the small folded card!

"Who'd you get?" asked my good buddy Mark.

"I don't think we're supposed to say."

My calm, confident demeanor served as a protective shield. But why was one needed? After all, presents had a five dollar limit and the giver remained anonymous. An ingenious system, devised to accomplish two important results: 1) to protect the identities of kids who brought really lame gifts, and 2) to protect someone like me, whose buddies would unleash unending ridicule for having to get something for a girl, especially Lori. Yes, fifth-graders will unfairly and unnecessarily judge a person based on a gift's perceived value and intent. Many never outgrow that inclination.

Yet the real drama surrounding my draw of Lori's name was still ahead.

When students wrote their names on small cards, they had also scribbled an idea or two to help their secret Santa. When I told my mom we needed to buy a present, I laughed when I said, "Her card says 'a piece of candy.' Doesn't she know that's nowhere near five dollars? She's so weird."

But Mom had an idea and told me she'd take care of it. Her creative wheels were already turning.

Before I left for school the day of the party, she gave me a plastic bag with Lori's gift neatly wrapped. "What did we get her?" I asked.

"What she asked for."

When I walked into class, I waited until no one watched to put Lori's nice looking gift on the pile—no sense in having someone trace me based on the fancy department-store paper my mom preferred for Christmas gifts. Finally,

I could relax and look forward to the snacks and whatever secret Santa had for me.

Midway through the party that afternoon, after the first round of snacks and games, we sat at our desks for the gift exchange. The teacher called names in alphabetical order for us to find our gifts and open them in front of the class. When Lori's turn came I acted uninterested, keeping a low profile at my desk several feet from the gift table. Close enough, though, to see the look of shock and delight on Lori's face when she tore the wrapping off a box of expensive chocolates! The kind in individual foils and loaded with peanuts and caramel. She received, by far, the best gift of the day. *Oh Mom, how could you? Don't let it show; act surprised.*

Our class went quiet as she made strange but happy sounds. Then everyone cheered. *What a great idea, Mom!* For a moment, Lori stood on the other end of the social order. Without a doubt, the best end.

I, though, sat there and said nothing. Why would I? Up to this point, all this was my mom's idea. But I still joined the joy. Lori's smile brightened the entire room; for a moment, she ventured outside the bubble and life was as it should be—for her and for all of us. Loneliness is so prevalent, yet so easily remedied.

Then, in typical unnoticeable fashion, she returned to her seat. After the rest of us collected our gifts, we lined up at the table that held our second round snacks. There's nothing like a frosted brownie to end the last day of school before Christmas break.

When I returned to my desk, I nearly dropped that brownie and my cup of Hi-C. At some point in the previous couple of minutes, when no one (including me) watched, Lori had placed a chocolate-covered peanuts and caramel piece of candy, in its individual foil, on my desk. I quickly scanned the other desks. No candy anywhere. Wide-eyed and nearly hyperventilating, I slowly turned and looked left three rows and back four desks to where Lori sat. Fear's claw gripped my throat as I pictured her gnarled-teeth smile coming back at me. What if she thought I liked her? After all, the only time these boxes of chocolate appear is on Valentine's Day. *Why, Mom, did you do this to me?* But Lori did not smile. Instead, she acted uninterested and kept a low profile—simply looking at her box of fancy chocolates as she ate a piece.

That day, my paranoia blocked my ability to see what truly took place. A brief moment, noticed by no one other than her and me, displayed the quiet goodness in her heart as much as it indicted the crusty condition of my own. Her response, or lack thereof, still insists on my attention today.

Off and on I watched her the remaining twenty minutes until we left for the day. She shared a fancy chocolate with no one else. It appeared that she ate only one, gave one away, and then took the box home.

How did she know it was me? Her gesture, placing a chocolate covered peanuts and caramel on my desk, acted as her way of saying "thank you" for the gift, the joy, or maybe the chance, for once, to feel noticed for a good reason. What remains baffling, though, is that even though she could hardly write her name and never completed a test or quiz, in an instant she discerned what our brightest classmates never figured out. She knew who gave her the gift. And she thanked me for it, the very kid who openly winced when forced to take her as the last pick for kickball teams.

Oh, if I could just take back those looks, the mean comments, and the laughter I either led or joined. Unfortunately, that's impossible. I didn't even deserve the appreciation; my mom did. But when Lori put the piece of candy on my desk, for what seemed like the first time in my life I, too, received notice for a good reason.

The richest, most enduring and life-changing lesson I've ever learned came from a girl when she said absolutely nothing. It just took a while to achieve full effect. Makes me wonder why the expectation exists that life change takes place instantaneously.

This story is less about me showing up in Lori's life than it is about Lori showing up in mine. She taught me to give a box-of-chocolate effort for other people, especially when all that's expected is a piece of candy. Doubly true when the person who receives it sits last on the list of people who expect to receive something unexpectedly good. The almost half century that her smile and squeal have stayed intact in my memory proves to me that doing something for someone else without the need for notice leaves a lasting mark. She helped me understand that the joy of making someone feel special easily trumps any self-consciousness about what others might think.

Most of all, Lori demonstrated that extending good-ness—making a difference—requires no power, prestige, or popularity. And that those coveted luxuries might actually stand in the way.

We never talked about the piece of chocolate; she never brought it up and neither did I. I'd like to say we became good friends, but we didn't. Our family moved to another state 18 months later. Lori passed away a couple years after that.

Looking back at that moment now, I struggle to recall the names and faces of anyone else in my fifth-grade class. Lori, though, remains the one person I remember well. Her graciousness serves as my inspiration to serve others and to make conscious efforts to actually earn that piece of candy. I just never quite feel that I do.

The truth is that a simple, single act of goodness can ripple across many years and touch many lives when it ignites something—maybe passion—in a person's heart. Guilt doesn't last that long. Neither do good intentions. That's what happened to my heart. Every so often, oh how I wish more regularly, the flames kick in. So I dance with a wheelchair-bound boy, shed tears with a three-year-old Haitian, and eat pie every week with a World War II veteran. Along the way, I notice the heavy volume of heaven-on-earth moments when people lend a hand, share a word, or somehow show up for someone else—and return life to be as it should be. *Thank you, Lori.*

"I've got something for you," Lou said. "Over there, it's on the table."

"Thanks, Lou, these look great," I replied as I picked up a box of fancy chocolates. "Do you want one?"

"Nah. Take the box with you today as my gift. But don't just put it away somewhere. Either eat 'em or give 'em away, but don't forget about them."

"I'll remember, I promise."

And let us consider how we may spur one another on toward love and good deeds.

MUCH LOVE AND APPRECIATION TO...

Becky for your fierce, passionate belief in me and this book.

Scott for the amazing relationship we share and inspiration to always keep going.

Erin for joy, smiles, laughter, and all the wonderful life moments you create.

Abbie for joining all the fun; welcome!

Judy for your steadfast partnership and friendship. Big hug.

Troy for believing, and for your hard work on my behalf; a true blessing.

Adam and Stan for your willingness to take a chance.

TC8 Small Group *for a journey of the heart that changed me. A lot.*

Watermark Life Group *for the laughs, the moments, the reality.*

Kids Hope USA Staff and Board *for flexibility, support, and the passion to do something worth doing.*

Bob *for the affirming words and thoughts that gave life— to this book and me.*

Doug, Phil, and Mark *for wisdom, encouragement, and the precious gift of time.*

Becky (once again)—*for the moment you showed up and changed my life for the better; in fact, you changed it for good. Real love does that.*

ABOUT THE AUTHOR

David Staal currently serves as president of Kids Hope USA, a fast-growing national non-profit organization that partners local churches with local elementary schools. Kids Hope USA trains churches to provide mentors for at-risk students, and is America's largest faith-based mentoring program.

Staal began his career in corporate marketing. After thirteen years in the business world, he became the communications director for Willow Creek Community Church. This role involved hands-on leadership for Willow's publications and creative design areas, as well as serving as the church's spokesperson. Following this assignment he served as children's ministry director until his departure for Kids Hope USA.

Staal has published five previous titles, all through Harper Collins Christian Publishing / Zondervan:

- *Lessons Kids Need to Learn* (2012)

- *Words Kids Need to Hear* (2008)

- *Leading Kids to Jesus* (2006);

- *Leading Your Child to Jesus* (2006)

- *Making Children's Ministry the Best Hour of Every Kid's Week* (2004); co-authored with Sue Miller

A graduate of Purdue University in West Lafayette, Indiana, he holds a BA in Communications and has completed several Executive Education courses through the University of Michigan Business School and the University of Chicago Business School. He lives in Grand Haven, MI, with his wife Becky. There, he is involved in various community activities, including serving as board chairman of Grand Valley State University's Kirkhof College of Nursing. David and Becky have two adult children; a son Scott (married to Abbie), and a daughter Erin.